954.02

Moore, Russell

Thailand-Malaysia-Singapore

C158

WALKERTON PUBLIC LIBRARY
WALKERTON, INDIANA

THAILAND • MALAYSIA • SINGAPORE

THAILAND
MALAYSIA
SINGAPORE

PEOPLE • PLACES • HISTORY

by

Russell F. Moore

WALKERTON PUBLIC LIBRARY
WALKERTON, INDIANA

THAI-AMERICAN PUBLISHERS

NEW YORK

Copyright © 1975 by Russell F. Moore

All rights reserved
including the right of reproduction
in whole or in part in any form

Library of Congress Catalog Card Number: 74-27959

Manufactured in the United States of America

For Shelby

CONTENTS

Photo Credits

Photographs used in Chapter 3 were reproduced with permission of the Tourist Organization of Thailand. The Malaysian Tourist Development Corporation supplied the photos used in Chapter 4. The illustrations in Chapter 5 were supplied by the Singapore Tourist Promotion Board. Copyright of the original photos is reserved by the Board.

ACKNOWLEDGMENTS

The author is indebted to a number of people who helped make the appearance of this book possible. I am especially obligated to Sunan Watcharanantakul, who, with infinite patience, never failed to supply answers to the many questions which I posed concerning this or that matter relating to his country and people. He also provided the maps and sketches.

I have to thank Mr. Pannara Choochan, Chief of Publicity Section of the Tourist Organization of Thailand, and Ms. How Pack Chin, Promotion Officer of the Singapore Tourist Promotion Board, who arranged for my use of many of the photographs which appear in the book. Mr. Boonchai Kasivate, of the Thai Ministry of Industry, placed several publications at my disposal which were of great value in treating of the cultural aspects of his country. Mr. Philip Wong was most helpful in getting me around Singapore and was kind enough to read and comment on the portion of the manuscript dealing with that country.

To the many others who in one way or another assisted and to my many Thai friends who encouraged me in the writing of the book, I extend heartfelt thanks.

R.F.M.

New York
Winter 1974

INTRODUCTION

This is a book about three countries in Southeast Asia: Thailand, Malaysia and Singapore. There is no particular logic to the fact that the three are treated within the covers of a single volume. Their cultures and historical development are quite different. Something might be said to the effect that all three have resisted the tide of Communism in this part of the world and exist as free nations living outside the Communist orbit, relatively untroubled by the strife which has raged for so long in neighboring Vietnam, Laos and Cambodia.

Each country has been treated in tripartite fashion. First the land itself is described, its physical characteristics, climate and geography, and some characteristics of the people who inhabit the land are detailed. Then the historical background of each nation has been briefly sketched. Finally, there is an account of some of the interesting places that attract the traveler's attention on a visit to these areas.

Here and there the author has referred to Thailand as Siam. The names are used more or less interchangeably. In 1939 the Thais changed the name of their country from Siam to Thailand, which means literally "land of the free." The original name, Siam or "Syam", is very old and has been found in Vietnam and Angkor Wat inscriptions dating from the 11th and 12th centuries.

The reader should also be forewarned that there are several ways of spelling some Thai names in English. An effort has been made to use the simplest spellings possible, most often the phonetic spelling, and in the case of place names such spellings as will be found on good contemporary maps in English.

Chapter 1

THAILAND:
LAND AND PEOPLE

Thailand means literally "land of the free." It is also a "calm" land. The concept of *Chai yen,* the "cool heart," is the ideal of the Thai, who generally seeks an atmosphere of tranquility in his daily life and affairs. The common expression, *Mai pen rai* ("never mind"), gets the Thai over the minor frustrations and annoyances of daily life and helps to preserve his cheerful, casual nature. The people are cheerful and easygoing, hospitable by nature, and friendly. They tend to be conservative in outlook, and have an ingrained respect for authority and a deep reverence for the monarchy. The Buddhist heritage has produced a gentle people.

It is a land of contentment. The climate poses no hardship. There is rice in the fields, fish in the water. Farmer folk own eighty per cent of the cultivated land, and about eighty per cent of the population live in small villages. Excluding Bankok, which is the country's only metropolitan center, there are no more than a dozen cities with more than 30,000 inhabitants.

In the country the farmer's house is typically constructed of wood. Very possibly it will be of unvarnished teak. It consists of a platform on stilts, several feet above the ground, with two or three rooms and a verandah. The walls are often of plaited bamboo, and the roof is thatched with palm. The outside ladder or staircase probably has an uneven number of steps as some believe that this prevents unwanted spirits from entering the dwelling. In some of the village houses the supports may be of iron, and, particularly if

1

the house has two storeys, the supports may rest in concrete. The first floor may have brick walls, and the second may be of wood rather than bamboo. Suburban bungalow dwellings are likely to be of quite modern design, and for the affluent in the cities there are substantial, air-conditioned homes very often with attractive gardens.

Temperatures are likely to be somewhere between 85 and 90 degrees (F.) much of the year. Temperatures below 64 degrees or above 100 degrees (F.) are most uncommon. The tropical monsoon climate prevails. "Monsoon" refers to a seasonal wind. It is the moisture-laden southwest monsoon, sweeping in from the Indian Ocean in late May, that brings the torrential downpours of the rainy season, which extends from early June to October. It is particularly humid during this period. Cooler weather comes in November and continues through February. The dry season extends from December through April, when the prevailing winds come in from the northeast, and from February to May it is especially hot.

Thailand covers an area of about 200,000 square miles. More than half of the country is still covered by forests. There are four distinctive regions. The vast central plain contains a little more than 30% of the population; the continental highlands are in the north; to the northeast is the Korat Plateau; and in the south there is the peninsula. Half of the rice produced in Thailand comes from the central plain. The great Menam Chao Phraya, the "lord of rivers," flows through the area, and the heavy clay soil on the plain produces large crops of cassava, corn (maize) and castor beans as well as rice. Natural rainfall is supplemented by irrigation water, and the area is crossed by an extensive system of klongs. These klongs, or canals, provide not only for irrigation and drainage, but they are filled with fish, which is a staple in the diet, and they are used for transportation, for bathing and for drinking water. The central plain, with Bangkok (Krung Thep) in its center, is really the heartland of the country.

The irrigation water for the central plain comes down from the highlands of the north. The northern region embraces about a third of the area of the country, and here peanuts, corn, kapok and ramie are the important crops. The teak forests are here too, and elephants may be seen handling the great teak logs. Although their numbers steadily decrease there are still some wild elephants, and now and again Himalayan bear as well as tigers and leopards are sighted in the forested northern highlands.

Northeast Thailand contains roughly a third of the total land area and also about a third of the population. Sandy soils and uncertain rainfall tend to reduce agricultural output. Even so, about 30 percent of total rice production comes from this region, and the area leads in the production of jute, kenaf and other fibres used in the manufacture of gunnysacks and for export.

Peninsular Thailand in the south is almost blanketed with rain forest. The area receives rainfall from both the northeast and southwest monsoons, and in this part of the country it is hot much of the time. Most of the country's natural rubber and virtually all of the tin comes from this area. There are mangrove swamps along the Gulf coast and in the streams running down to the coast there are innumerable crocodiles. In the tropical rain forest there is seemingly an infinite number of different kinds of trees. Among them are gigantic yang trees, with tops so dense with foliage as to nearly shut out the sunlight. There are pines, great clumps of bamboo, giant ferns and vines and rattans entwining the tree trunks. Lower down one sees many orchids and thick moss on fallen tree trunks. Animal life here seems equally varied: tigers and panthers, small deer, tapirs, gibbons, monkeys, flying squirrels, lizards, more than fifty different kinds of snakes, leeches, and innumerable butterflies.

Thailand is not overpopulated. The country now has a population of about 36 million. Bangkok, including Thonburi, has two and one-half million inhabitants. The Thais are a remarkably homogenous people. There are several minority groups, but these, wherever possible, are being assimilated. The more than three million Chinese in Thailand comprise the largest ethnic minority. Half of these ethnic Chinese, i.e. those following Chinese customs and speaking the language, live in and around Bangkok. Most of the rest are in other population centers where they are active in business pursuits. The ethnic Malaysians live mostly in the four southern provinces. They number around three-quarters of a million and have been slower to assimilate. The Indian-Pakistani minority is declining in numbers. Among other groups are those of Cambodian descent, Vietnamese, Mons, Shans, the indigenous Sui, and people of the hill tribes in the far north and west (the Meo, Karen, Yao and Lisus). Outside of the ethnic groups there are

Thais of mixed Chinese and Thai ancestry, and in the extreme south part of the country there are many people of mixed Malay-Thai blood.

The economy of Thailand is basically agricultural. Some 85-90 per cent of the people are farmers, and, incidentally, the majority own their own land. About 76 per cent of all arable land is planted in rice, and the production of rice is central to the economy.

When the first rains come in May or June, the farmer begins to prepare his rice field for sowing. Five or six weeks later the entire family transplant the seedlings from their starter bed to the fields. Tractors would be quite useless in the sticky mud of the rice fields, but water buffalo (of which there are seven million in the country) are ideal, and five or six million oxen also work on the farms. In four or five months, the dry season and harvest time arrive. The rice is harvested, threshed and finally sold, probably to a Chinese paddy merchant. Much of the production is moved along the klongs to mills or storage depots.

Thailand is in first place as an exporter of rice, in second place in the production of tin ore, and a third major export is teakwood. Exports in the order of their importance are rice, rubber, tin and teak.

The teak is a tall straight tree with large oval-shaped leaves. Its white blossoms appear in July. Once the tree is felled and the log formed, it is maneuvered by trained elephants to whatever means of transportation is utilized to get the logs to the lumber mill. Years ago the teak logs were floated down the rivers from the forest areas to Bangkok and the mills. They were often lashed together to form rafts, and it might take two, three, even four years for the logs to reach Bangkok where they were sold and cut. Nowadays there are dams or other obstructions on the rivers, so that logs are most likely to go by rail.

In addition to these major exports, other agricultural products include corn, kenaf, cassava, cotton, soybeans, tobacco, sugar cane, peanuts, castor beans, sesame, coconuts, pepper, jute and ramie. Many varieties of bananas are grown as well as oranges, limes, tangerines, mango, breadfruit, papaya, jackfruit, rambutan, sapodilla, litchi and numerous other fruits and vegetables.

While some lands in the northeast are suitable for grazing and there is some production of cattle and hogs, most of the output is consumed in the domestic market and has no export significance. There is no dairy cattle industry.

There are fish in abundance in the waters. Gulf fishermen bring in catches of mackerel, herring and anchovies and there are also sole, pomfret, mullet and bass. The tropical shark is another salt water prize, valued not least of all for its fins which are widely used in the preparation of Chinese dishes. Inland fresh waters, the rivers, klongs, lakes and sometimes even the flooded rice fields, yield carp, catfish, perch, gourami and murrals among others. Fish and rice are the two staples in the national diet.

The Thai government has made vast strides in expanding the nation's economy since World War II. The construction of new all-weather highways has opened up new markets and, especially in the northeast, has enabled farmers to increase their incomes because they can now get crops to markets which they previously could not reach.

American economic aid has built several highways and hundreds of bridges, equipped hospitals, trained teachers, and contributed to hydro-electric and flood-control projects. Such aid has not taken the form of spectacular projects, as is so often the case with the Soviets, but has provided basic, long-continuing improvements.

The irrigation network has been expanded, and several hydro-electric projects are now supplying electricity to the provinces and meeting industrial needs which have increased sharply in the past decade. The great Bhumibol Dam, now nearly completed, will supply electricity to nearly 40 provinces and irrigate several hundred thousands of acres of land. The Sirikit Dam, now under construction, will provide power in the northeast and there are numerous other projects in various parts of the country which, along with the new roads, will boost incomes and the standard of living in these areas.

Religion and Culture

The Thais are a religious people, and Thailand is a Buddhist nation. Considerably more than 90 per cent of the Thai ethnic group profess Buddhism, which should perhaps be obvious from the fact that there are at least 20,000 Buddhist wats (temple-monastery complexes) in the country, 250 of them in Bangkok alone. Buddhist belief permeates the life of the individual from cradle to grave. The village wat is the center of community life. The saffron robe of the monk carries with it high prestige, and the order of Buddhist monks is a social institution of great importance in Thai society.

Most young Thai men, usually in their early twenties, spend a brief period in a wat as monks. They are free to enter when they please and equally free to leave when they please. Some spend only a week or two. Others remain for longer periods, or may even spend the rest of their lives as monks. The young man has his head and eyebrows shaved, is provided with a saffron robe and bowl for food, and enters the monastery where he lives an austere existence bordered by a number of rules of conduct. His needs, as well as those of all the other monks, are met by the Buddhist custom of providing for their food, robes and other essentials. The Buddhist believes that he gains merit when he feeds a monk, or helps build a new wat, or performs some other religious act. Accumulated merit, under Buddhist doctrine, assures a better life in future reincarnations.

Buddhism is least of all doctrinaire, and in its practice there are some Brahmanic rituals, in the marriage ceremony and in ceremonies of state, for example, and especially on the popular level there is a primitive animism, a spirit worship that is older than the Thais themselves. In remote parts of the country Buddhism is a veneer laid over earlier animistic beliefs. Spirits abound in the religious practice of the average Thai and must be propitiated by prayers and offerings.

Thus the householder is certain to provide a little spirit house for the spirit of the land (*Phra Phum Chao Thi*) upon which he has built his dwelling. That is not to say that either animism or Brahminism, per se, are practiced as religions by Buddhists, only that some elements of these remain to color Buddhism.

Buddhism came to Thailand from India and Ceylon at about the time of Christ, give or take a century or two. Archaeological evidence confirms its presence by the 6th century A.D. and some scholars believe that it reached Thailand as early as 300 B.C. The faith is believed to have first come to Nakhon Pathom, about 30 miles west of Bangkok, which was then the center of the kingdom of Dvaravati. From this Indianized kingdom it spread to surrounding areas, and later the Burmese extended the Buddhist teachings into the areas they conquered. In the north and east the Khmers ruled and followed their own interpretation of Hinduism. When the Thais migrated from southern China they brought along their own animistic beliefs. They adopted the local Buddhist religion and elements of Hinduism while still retaining their animism, so that today popular Buddhism contains these other elements.

Buddhism traces its founding to the life and teachings of Siddhartha Gautama, born the son of a tribal chief in what is now Nepal, in northern India, about 563 B.C. The young prince was shielded in early life from the poverty and miseries of the common people. One day as he was passing through a village he saw a sick man, a very old man, and a dead man. He was deeply moved by the experience. According to the Hindu belief, such suffering and misery must be repeated through endless reincarnations. Although now 29 years old, married and a father, he renounced his title as a prince, his family, his wealth and went out alone into the world to seek a meaning for these things.

He found no key to these mysteries in Hindu mysticism and, ultimately, so tradition has it, he seated himself under a great tree (the Bodhi tree, or tree of wisdom) resolved to meditate until he could find the truth. After long meditation, he gained insight into the truth. This was the moment of his Enlightenment! Life is suffering. Suffering is caused by desire. To escape suffering, therefore, a man must conquer his desires. This he can do by leading a life of perfect goodness. When this state is reached, there is no more desire, hence no suffering. Enlightenment is attained, a state of pure bliss in which the individual is freed of human ego and worldly concepts of sorrow and pain, evil, even life and death themselves, have no meaning.

Siddhartha was now the Buddha – the Enlightened One. During his remaining years he traveled through India preaching the principles of his new-found wisdom.

He taught that all things change. Change results from the law of *Karma*, i.e., from the law of cause and effect. Within this relationship of change, man can determine his own salvation. Good deeds and bad deeds decide a man's future state in subsequent reincarnations. It is only through the cultivation of virtues and innumerable reincarnations that one can ultimately attain Nirvana (Enlightenment). In terms of a practical code of morality, the Buddhist must not lie or steal, commit adultery, indulge in intoxicants, or kill living creatures.

In brief essentials, the Buddha taught the Four Noble Truths: life consists of suffering; suffering results from desire; cessation of desire results in cessation of suffering and rebirth; this end can be attained by following the Eightfold Path. The Eightfold Path consists of Right Understanding; Right Purpose; Right Speech; Right Action; Right Livelihood; Right Effort; Responsiveness to Truth; Contemplation. The three great principles are that nothing is permanent, life consists of suffering, and the soul is illusion.

After the death of the Buddha his followers divided into two schools. The orthodox school is that of *Therevada* Buddhism (the doctrine of the Elders), which holds to the original teachings from the traditional Pali scriptures and admits of the efficacy of individual effort in attaining salvation. This school is also referred to as Hinayana Buddhism, or "Lesser Vehicle" Buddhism. Therevadism is the dominant belief in Thailand, Ceylon, Burma and Laos. *Mahayana* ("Greater Vehicle") Buddhism became dominant in the north, in China, Japan, Korea and Vietnam. It adopted a more liberal interpretation of the Buddha's teachings and enlarged them into relatively complex philosophical and theological systems.

In so many ways Buddhism, in its purist sense, is as much a philosophy as it is a religion. The Buddha did not preach the existence of any deity. He was himself a teacher, not a god. It is not faith, but following in the path of the Buddha that leads to Nirvana. Nor is there anything supernatural in Therevada Buddhism. On its popular level, of course, it is practiced as a religion, with liturgy, priesthood, and millions of devoted followers who gain spiritual renewal and a deep emotional experience from their worship. In everyday terms, the Buddhist seeks ever to improve himself by making and storing up merit (*tam boon*) to improve his chances in his next life. Common ways of gaining merit include such activities as attending temple services on *Wan Phra* (Buddhist Sunday), feeding a monk, charity to the poor, gilding a Buddha image, helping to construct a temple, reciting scriptures.

While Buddhism is overwhelmingly in first place as the religion of the land, there are other religions and religious institutions in the country, all graciously tolerated.

Thai Art and Culture

Buddhism is at the very core of Thai culture, and Thai art is primarily religious in nature. It possesses a unique style but one which reflects numerous influences arising from varied contacts with other cultures during the long course of Thai history. The Indian and Chinese are two major influences, and to these have been added borrowings from the Khmers of Cambodia, the Srivijayan kingdom of Sumatra and the Mons of Dvaravati.

The complexities of these borrowings and mergings of different cultures, the details of which are still conjectural in many areas, are beyond the scope of these few pages. The Thai culture that has emerged, however, is distinctly Thai. Sometimes, as in the case of the language, words borrowed originally from the Khmers and made a part of the Thai language, for example, were later borrowed back in their Thai versions by the Khmers and made a part of the vocabulary of the latter language. There was thus a cultural exchange.

The Thais migrated from southern China at different times and settled in various areas further to the south. For a long time they were in contact with the Chinese, and in their movement southward brought with them elements of the Chinese culture. There are in the Thai language, for example, several hundred words which are common to the Chinese language. Some classes of words may even have come into both languages from an earlier common source. Later Chinese influence in Thai art is noticeable in the use of bright colors in architectural works, in lacquer work, porcelain and mother-of-pearl pieces.

Early Thai settlements in the Chao Phraya basin, in what is now central Thailand, were within the territory of the Khmer empire. Here, again, Thai culture was enriched by Khmer influence which is readily noted in certain architectural examples, among others. The empire of the Khmers was hinduized and at times Northern Buddhist, thus exposing the development of a strictly Thai culture to these influences. As Khmer power declined, the Thais in a very real sense inherited much from the culture of their former masters.

With the founding of the kingdoms of Sukhothai and Ayutthaya, the Thai peoples came into contact with the Mons, in what is now lower Burma, and their Southern Buddhistic culture. At the same time, when King Ramkhaeng of Sukhothai extended his kingdom into the Malay peninsula, there were contacts with the remnants of the Javanese-Sumatran empire of Srivijaya. To the far north and northwest, the Thais came into contact with a strong Burmese influence and distinctive cultural characteristics quite different from those elsewhere in the country.

At whatever period, from whatever people and to whatever extent Thai culture was influenced, it must again be emphasized that
a unique and distinctly Thai culture emerged.

The golden age of Thai civilization was the Sukhothai period,
and there is perhaps no better place to begin a brief look at this
era than a consideration of the Sukhothai image of the Lord Buddha. It was the greatest artistic creation of the age, and it gave
visual expression to the deep feeling the Thais had in their hearts
for the teachings of the Buddha as they were made known by
Hinayana Buddhism. Although surrounded by the Mahayana
Buddhism and Hinduism of their Khmer rulers, the Thais embraced
the Hinayana (Therevada) doctrine as best suited to their spiritual
needs and temperment.

Of the hundreds of thousands of Buddha images made in
Buddhist lands from Ceylon and India in the west to Japan in the
east, most possessed highly stylized features. To preserve authenti-
city, one image copied an earlier one, and that was a copy of one
earlier still. Because the object of the artist was solely to glorify
Buddha, the traditional Thai artist is anonymous. He was most
unlikely, in any event, to imbue his artistic creation with personal
eccentricities of style or workmanship. The creation of a new style
was possible only under such special circumstances as existed in
Sukhothai.

One factor contributing to this new style was the medium itself.
Until the 12th century most images of the Buddha and the Hindu
gods had been carved from stone. Coincident with the revival and
emergence of Hinduism as the predominant faith in India there was
a wide popular demand for small statues of the Hindu gods and
demi-gods. Bronze casting was widely employed in India and Ceylon in meeting the demand, and the technique was also known in
Thailand. While there were numerous bronze images in the Chieng-
saen style of northern Thailand, these were modeled after earlier
stone images. It remained for the Sukhothai artists to bring the
casting of Buddha images in bronze to its zenith of perfection and
create a style quite different from anything that had gone before.

The bronze casting technique permitted greater flexibility than
that ordinarily attained in working with more resistant stone. The
"lost wax" process was utilized. A model of clay and sand mixture
was first prepared and then given a heavy coat of wax. This wax
was modeled to create the form desired and was in turn coated

with the sand and clay mixture. When the completed model was then baked, the wax melted and was drained away. Molten metal was then poured into the form to replace the wax. The resulting image, with its sinuous lines and smooth surface texture, was ideally suited to convey the spiritual quality of the subject matter.

In viewing one of these exquisite creations, one is less conscious of the heavy bronze from which it is made than of the undulating, idealized form which seems in complete harmony with the spiritual concept which has been materialized. The faint smile on the Buddha's face suggests an inner peace and happiness that has come with victory over earthly passions. The several surviving examples by Sukhothai artists of the walking Buddha convey an impression of movement, and the hands are exquisitely modeled.

Other Buddha images by Sukhothai artists were modeled in stucco. Stucco was widely used in Khmer and Dvaravati arts as well. Because a modeling technique was utilized as in bronze casting, a rather similar style resulted.

Regrettably, practically nothing remains of Sukhothai painting. The little that can be studied affirms that it was two dimensional in character, as opposed to the three dimensional art of the West, and depends for its beauty on the expressiveness of the line. Such painting was in monochromatic red, white and black. Other early examples of Buddha paintings reflect the undulating, relaxed, graceful characteristics of the Sukhothai bronzes. The later art of Ayutthaya and northern Thailand was much influenced by Sukhothai. There is a magnificent example of the blending of north Thai and Sukhothai sculpture in the bronze image of a seated Buddha at the Wat Sutat in Bangkok.

The pottery produced at Sukhothai and in the kilns of Sawankaloke is outstanding for its balanced form and proportions. It is this fine form which brings out its beauty, since it is monochromatic and unembellished by the rich colors characteristic of the Bencharong ceramics which were made in Ayutthaya. Not only was pottery produced for a wide variety of personal and household uses, but the artisans also turned out ceramic roof tiles of typically bluish-green glaze, and a variety of architectural devices.

Thai classical architecture inevitably makes a powerful impression on the Westerner visiting the kingdom for the first time. It is so truly unlike anything anywhere else in the world and so distinctively Thai. Here again there were important early influences assimilated by the Thais, including those of the Dvaravati, the Srivijaya, Khmer, Burmese and even some direct Indian influence. To some extent these early influences were regional and today if one comes across a temple monument exhibiting strong Burmese influence it will most likely be in the west or northwest. In most instances such foreign characteristics as were absorbed in Thai classical architecture were so completely assimilated that geography is of no significance. Thus, early Thai temple architecture perpetuated the monochromatic practice of the Khmers, but this gave way later to the polychromatic style of the Chinese. Today the typical Buddhist wat, whether located in Chiang Mai in the north, Nakhon Si Thammarat in the south, or elsewhere in the country, is certain to present the brilliant gold gilding, reds and greens and other colors so characteristic of the Thai style.

The use of particular materials also added to the distinctive character of Thai architecture. In temple architecture the buildings are typically of wood with ornamental and decorative parts usually gilded and often further embellished with glass mosaic. The roofs are of terra-cotta glazed tiles of various colors. Stucco is used to decorate gables, and to provide ornaments for door and window frames and on various moldings. In later architectural periods bits of broken pieces of colored porcelain have been worked into ornamental patterns on exterior surfaces. Lacquer work and inlaid mother-of-pearl have been widely employed on window and door panels. Add brilliant tropical sunlight to the gold-leaf gilding, the chips of porcelain, the dark reds, greens, blues and violets, and a positively dazzling artistic effect is achieved.

If the physical materials of construction and decoration influenced the character of Thai architecture, of equal importance was the use to which structures were put. As already stated, the Thais inherited much of Khmer culture. Why, then, does Thai architecture vary so markedly from the Khmer style? In religious building the answer lies in the purposes for which the structures were used. The main hall in any Thai wat typically houses the Buddha image and is used by the monks for meditation and the performance of all of the important ceremonies incident to the practice of the Buddhist religion. It is called the *bot*, and it must be sufficiently large to accomodate a hundred or so monks and others who may participate in such activities. The Khmer temples contained relatively small square cells and narrow corridors easily roofed with the Khmer vaulting system. The latter was totally inadequate, however, for the wide spans which had to be roofed in Thai Buddhist temples. The typical stone roof of the Khmers was replaced in Thai practice with timber.

The lofty sloping roof of a bot is usually superimposed in several tiers, and at the end of each ridge of the roof there will usually be a graceful finial called a *chofa*. This may derive from the horn on ancient animistic masks or possibly it may be a simplified rendering of the "Markara" motif of the Sukhothai period. Note the sketch.

Chofa

Some additional remarks concerning the wats are contained in a later section, but brief mention will be made at this point of the *chedi*, which is the most revered of Buddhist religious structures. The chedi originally contained relics of the Lord Buddha and has now become the symbol of Buddhism much as the cross is venerated by Christians. The prototype of the chedi (*stupa*) came from central India. This classic type, as exemplified by the large chedi at Nakhon Pathom, is composed of a drum at the base, a dome shaped like a bell, surmounted by a chair symbolic of the seat of Buddha, and overall the *chatra*, or umbrella, which reaches skyward as a slender pinnacle. The northern type exhibits a cubical base with Buddha images in niches at its sides, and there may be one or several storeys between the cubical base and the dome. In this style there are often small chedis at the corners of the base.

The Thai language belongs to the same family of languages as the Chinese. It is primarily monosyllabic in the formation of words. There are many homonyms, i.e. words with the same sound but different meanings. In some cases differentiation in meaning is achieved by the use of different tones; otherwise the meaning is established by the context of the phrase or sentence in which it is used. Classifiers may also be prefixed to clarify the meaning of a word. The Thai alphabet is indirectly of Sanskrit origin and its present form was introduced in 1283 A.D. by the Sukhothai king Ramkhaeng. Consonants are written on a line from left to right. Marks above, below, before or after, indicate vowel sounds that follow them. In modern Thai there are 44 consonants representing 28 basic consonantal sounds. Writing is from left to right and spaces mark punctuation rather than word division. In speech, inflection is entirely lacking, and the language, like English, is phonetically eccentric.

There are several methods of transliterating Thai into English, none universally accepted. Accordingly, one Thai word may be spelled several different ways in English. If the word happens to be spelled phonetically, a further problem is added. Thus, phonetically, the name of a well-known figure in recent Thai history is *Sarit Thanarat*, but transliterated it is *Srisdi Dhanarajata*. To be fair to all systems, the author has been consistently inconsistent in matters of spelling!

The question of proper names also poses some difficulty for Westerners. It is only as recently as 1916 that the king decreed that Thais should take surnames. Going further back into Thai history one encounters such a problem as that posed by the names and titles of the first king of the present ruling dynasty. He was one of King Takh Sin's generals and was, before he became king, known as Chao Phraya Chakri. His real name was Tong-Duang, son of Phra Pinit Aksorn. As king he is known by the name Yodfah Chulaloke. He was crowned as Rama I. So it is that Tong-Duang, Chao Phraya Chakri, Yodfah Chulaloke and Rama I are one and the same person!

Traditional Thai literature deals primarily with religious themes— Buddhist or Hindu. Of central importance is the *Tripitaka* (the "Three Baskets"), which contains the doctrine of the Buddhist faith. It was originally written in Pali, said to be the language of the Buddha and also the language in which much of the sacred literature of India was written.

Thai writing probably originated with King Ramkhaeng's standardization of the characters of the alphabet. Sukhothai literature survives only in inscriptions, of which Ramkhaeng's stone inscription is the most famous, and in the *Traibhumikatha* which dates from 1345. The predominantly religious literature of the 15th and 16th centuries in the north is known through such surviving examples as the *Jinakalamali* (a history of Buddhism), a history of Lampoon state and a history of an early Buddha image brought to Siam from Ceylon. There are also some folktales extant from this period. All of these works are written in Pali.

It is difficult to assess the literature of the Ayutthaya period because so much was destroyed in the sack of the city in 1767. Of what did survive from the early period, mention might be made of the *Yuan Pai* (a story of the defeat of the Chiang Mai people), and the *Pra Lo* (a tragic romance). From the later Ayutthaya period, beginning with the reign of King Narai, a number of poetical works are known including the Buddhist poem written by King Sondharm with the title *Mahajati*. There are also a Siamese grammar, a history of Ayutthaya and some poetry by Pra Sri Mahosoth, among other works. A dance-drama, the romance of *Inao*, also dates from this period. It is based on the adventures of a Javanese hero-prince and is a classic of Thai literature. Among prose compositions of the period is the *Story of Nang Tantrai*, which was based on a tale from the *Arabian Nights*.

The destruction of the city and the annhiliation of the royal court make all the more remarkable the survival of these and some few other works of Ayutthayan literature. Printing was not introduced into the kingdom until later in the century so that at no time did many individual copies of these works exist.

After the restoration it was particularly during the first reign of the present dynasty (Rama I) that a strong effort was made to revive Thai culture. In the literary field the king ordered a concordance of the *Tripitaka* prepared, and a code of laws was compiled (the *Edition of the Three Seals*). He had a number of foreign classics translated into the Thai language. One of these was the *Sam Kok* a prose version of a Chinese historical romance of the Three Kingdoms (the *Sankuo*). Several histories of Buddhism in Siam were compiled, and the king himself wrote the *Ramakien*, one of the greatest classics in all of Thai literature. It retells the Indian legend of *Ramayana*, but it contains various episodes not to be found in the original epic.

In the second reign (Rama II) the king composed a new version of *Inao*, and the poet Suntorn Bhu authored *Phra Abhaimai*, a romantic tale in verse which, incidentally, sheds some light on the popular attitude in Thailand toward Europeans in the early part of the last century. The same author contributed to the writing of another well-known classic, the romance of *Khun Chang Khun*

Phen. This story, with its triangular love plot, has enjoyed great and continuing popular appeal, and for the interested reader it conveys as well a wealth of information concerning Thai social customs and beliefs prior to their being influenced by Western cultural attitudes.

With the reign of King Mongkut there came rapid development in prose fiction. Succeeding monarchs encouraged the retention of what was best in the old tradition but recognized as well as the new era of liberal thought in literature that got underway in the mid-19th century. Several rulers were especially gifted in the literary field and made significant contributions. King Chulalongkorn, for example, wrote the *Nidrajagrij*, which with Buradat's *Samaggibhed* and Suntorn's *Ilaraj*, constitutes some of the finest verse of the Bangkok period. Another ruler, Rama VI, translated several Shakespearean plays into Thai as well as works by Molière and other Western authors and playwrights.

Current literary output continues in the form of novels, religious histories, poetry and other prose works reflecting the many-faceted activities and aspirations of the Thai people.

Thai musical art is unique. It is difficult to compare with Western music. Thai musicians were traditionally trained orally by their teachers without benefit of written texts or musical scores. Melodies were learned and played by ear. Consequently, the corpus of traditional Thai music existed only in the memory of the musicians. The inevitable consequence has been that as music masters died, some of the older traditional works died with them.

Realizing that traditional Thai music was gradually disappearing, H.R.H. Prince Damrong Rajanubhab in 1929 inaugurated a most unusual program aimed at preserving such works by having them taken down in Western notation. A congress of music masters was convened, lists of compositions which had been maintained by the National Library were studied, and Phra Chen Duriyanga (a noted authority on Thai music) was given the task of devising a written system of notation capable of preserving this music as performed by a Piphat band. When it is recognized that no textbooks of musical theory existed, that there were no written instructions for the playing of the various musical instruments, and that many of the compositions on the Library lists were virtually unknown by living musicians, the magnitude of the task can be appreciated. There were technical obstacles, too, arising out of basic differences in the Western and Thai musical scales and similar considerations. The Thai musical scale, for example, is diatonic with neither major nor minor as in Western music. It consists of seven full tones in the octave without any semitones between the full tone-steps. In due course a great many works were written down and preserved for posterity. The undertaking was especially important in view of the strong impact that Western music has had on Thai musical development in recent years.

The Piphat band has two sections, one of woodwinds, the other of percussion instruments. The woodwind section consists of a single instrument, the *Pi Nai*, a cylindrical hollow tube of rosewood from which tones are produced by forcefully expelling air through a reed and controlling its flow with the fingers on a series

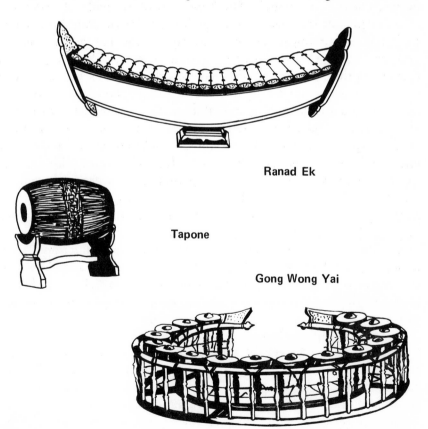

Ranad Ek

Tapone

Gong Wong Yai

of holes pierced in the body of the instrument. The piercing tone
of the Pi Nai is something like that produced by a bagpipe.

The melodic instruments in the percussion section include the
Ranad Ek, the *Ranad Thong Ek*, the *Ranad Thume* and the *Gong
Wong Yai*. The first three instruments consist of a resonance box,
each of slightly different design, made of seasoned hardwood or
teak. Resonance bars, positioned over the resonance chamber, are
made of hardwood or certain varieties of bamboo, and in the case
of the Ranad Thong Ek, of steel. They are played by striking the
bars with two beaters, much in the same manner as the xylophone
is played in the West. The Gong Wong Yai consists of resonant
metal disks, mostly of brass, with a concave embossing in the
center. They are suspended from an oval-shaped frame, of rattan or
cane, in the center of which the player is seated.

The rhythmic instruments of the percussion group consist of
drums, gongs and cymbals. The *Tapone* is often made of teakwood
in a bulging drum shape with parchment drawn over both ends.
Both hands and fingers are used to tap on the parchment ends to
produce some eleven different sound effects. The *Song Na* is
similar to the Tapone. It also has two drum heads but is a little
longer and more slender in form. The *Klong Thad* is a third form
of drum and the largest in use. Both ends are covered with parchment, but it is placed in a standing position and only the top drum
head is used in playing. Heavy bamboo sticks are used for the loud
notes and smaller, padded drumsticks for softer ones. The drum is
slightly tilted when it is in use to permit the lower parchment to
vibrate freely. The Klong Thad is used in twos or threes, never
singly. The *Gong Hooi* consists of a set of three circular gongs
suspended from a frame. It is purely an accessory instrument and
used only in presenting certain compositions, primarily those used
in staging the *Ramakien*. The *Charb Lek, Charb Yai* and *Ching* are
all types of cymbals. The latter are small, thick, cup-shaped
cymbals which set the tempo for the band. The Thai band has no
conductor.

A typical Piphat band consists of five to seven pieces. In
presenting a Thai classical dance in the country, it is not uncommon for the musical accompaniment to consist of a single Ranad,
perhaps two. Music is not used in Buddhist worship, but it may
be allowed in certain ceremonies and on festive occasions.

Thai classical dancing is so relatively well-known, even in the

West, that it requires little elaboration here. Suffice it to say that the dancers begin their training in childhood. The girls perform the male parts in the dance as well, because they are considered to be more graceful than boy dancers, and it is the graceful movements of the hands and arms, each with a special meaning, that are the very essence of the classic dance. Elaborate costumes, rich in color and design, and impressive golden head pieces are worn. The dances are typically based on various mythical legends. Whatever may be said of some of the other indigenous art forms, the classical dance retains its general popularity among the Thais as it has for centuries past.

Two other examples from the vast cultural heritage of the Thais may be less familiar to Western readers. These are the *Nang* or "shadow play," and the *Khon*, or "masked play," which latter is a form of the classic dance. There is some reason to believe that the Khon may have evolved from the Nang, so the latter will be first briefly mentioned.

The origins of the shadow play were probably in ancient India. There is a reference to such a form of play in a very old Buddhist text, and the *Mahabharata* contains references to exhibitions of hide figures on screens of cloth. Present scholarly research supports the view that the Siamese shadow play came to Thailand from India via the Sumatran Srivijaya Empire. Whatever elaboration the Nang may have received in Java and elsewhere, the Thai version originally retained only the story of Rama as its central theme with the addition of some episodes identified with local tradition. Much later other stories were screened as shadow plays. One of these, popular in the mid-18th century, was the romance of the Javanese hero, Panji.

While the word "Nang" connotes the shadow play, it is strictly translated as "hide figures." It was these hide figures which were projected, with back lighting, on a white cloth screen to provide the action of the play. The figures were made of cowhide. The hide was cured, smoothed and dried, and then polished. An artist would draw the desired figure on the hide — Rama, Sita, a demon king, mythical figures, or whatever else the story required — and then parts of the design were cut out. Light passing through these portions cast a shadow outline of the figure to be represented. Hides were often elaborately designed with scenic backgrounds of palaces, mountains or celestial scenes added to the central character or characters being represented. In addition to those prepared for the strictly shadow play, the hide figures were sometimes painted in bright colors for use in day performances. The figures were supported by two poles which enabled the manipulator, behind the screen, to move them about as the action of the story required.

In a presentation of a shadow play the manipulators and musicians assemble at about dusk. The hides are arranged by "sets" so that they can be readily located in the order in which they are to appear in the play. There are preliminary ceremonies to the accompaniment of music, the reciter pronounces the invocations, and the torches are lighted. The musicians strike up a march, and the reciters, who tell the story, and the manipulators, who provide the action on the screen, commence the play.

As the action proceeds, the manipulators bend and sway in time with the music as they move the hide figures about on the screen and strike poses consistent with the character being portrayed. To some extent the hide figure does little more than identify the role being portrayed. The action is necessarily supplied by the manipulator. It is now believed that this circumstance eventually led the manipulators to discard the hide figures entirely, and, coming out before the screen, perform the action of the play themselves. It is known that the first masked plays, were presented before a screen. The presence of the screen would seem to be evidence of the transition from shadow play to masked play.

The screening of the Nang usually terminated at midnight. However, sometimes in the present day a modern adaptation of the shadow play offered in rural areas, not with the classical *Ramakien* theme but with a modern motif, may last the entire night. What with competition from television, motion pictures and Western dance bands, it cannot truthfully be said that many young Thais are sitting up nights before shadow play screens. This art form, however, occupies an important place in the cultural history of the Thai people and surely merits the continuing study that it is receiving.

The most important characteristic of the Thai classical dance called the Khon is the wearing of masks by the performers. The masks identify the roles of the individual dancers. Traditionally all of the performers wore masks, however in recent times those taking the roles of humans and celestial beings may not do so. Sometimes, too, female demons may perform unmasked but with demon features painted upon their faces. Particular colors were assigned to the several roles. The facial mask of Rama was always green, the mask for Lakshman, yellow, and the mask for Bhrot was red.

Because the performers were masked, they could not speak, and the narrative of the story was provided by a reciter or chorus. Even in those cases in modern times where a performer wears no mask, he remains mute. The recitations are in poetic form or in what is best described as "rhythmic prose," which is used for dialogue and when it is necessary to describe the action taking place on the stage. There must be close coordination among performers, reciters and orchestra. The recitation has to be carefully fit into the timing of the dancers' movements, and vice versa.

The orchestra traditionally consisted of but five pieces, but nowadays it may have more. The *ranad* player serves as leader of the orchestral accompaniment. Also in recent times, the chorus may be augmented by the addition of extra singers, especially when the Khon is presented as a Court mask-play.

The story of the Khon is that of the *Ramakien*. As mentioned elsewhere, this is the Thai version of Valmiki's Hindu epic, the *Ramayana*. This Thai version was not derived directly from the original epic, however, but was patterned on an Indonesian version current in the age of the Srivijaya empire. The story exists in several versions, but so far as the masked play is concerned the two written by Rama I and Rama II are the ones used. It is a long story, and it is therefore customarily presented in episodes, e.g., "The Conquest of the Demon-crow," "The Fire Ordeal of Sita," "Maiyarab the Magician," etc.

In the Thai version, Rama wages war on Tosakanth, the demon king. The latter has abducted Sita, Rama's consort, and taken her to the island of Langka off the south coast of India. Rama and his brother Lakshman follow in pursuit. The aid of Hanuman, the monkey-god, is enlisted, and after a long seige and several battles with the demons Rama's armies are victorious. Tosakanth is killed, and Rama returns with his beloved Sita.

Chapter 2

THE THAIS IN HISTORY

The Thai people are believed to have originally come from the Altai Mountains in North Mongolia. They emigrated eastward to the fertile valleys of the Yellow River in China, where excavations indicate that they arrived as early as 1450 B.C. In later migrations they moved on, first to the area of the Huang-Ho River mouth and into the northern part of Sze-Chuan province, and then into the Yang-tse River basin.

Here they were in contact with the Chinese, who were moving into the area in increasing numbers. In about 843 B.C. the Tartars attacked the Thais at Lung, and in succeeding centuries the latter were periodically in conflict with the Chinese. In small groups they continued to make their way further south. This migration extended over a period of some five centuries.

There is evidence to indicate that the independent kingdom of Nanchao, in Yünnan, which emerged in the middle of the seventh century, was Thai. The Chinese historian Ma Tuan-Lin, writing in the 13th century, sheds invaluable light on the development of the Thai people during this period. The Thais were scattered about south of the Yang-tse and maintained an independent existence in at least six petty kingdoms of which there is a record. These in due course were united under Nanchao. At its zenith of power the kingdom extended over Annam and Tongking, into present day Burma and Laos, and to the borders of Sze-Chuan and Tibet.

The kings of Nanchao had to defend their land from the Tartars and Chinese. Tibet, on the west, was sometimes ally, sometimes foe. By the end of the eighth century the kingdom had passed under Chinese suzerainty, and by 1000 A.D. it had been reduced to the status of a tributary state. Finally, in 1253, the Thais lost what little independence they had maintained under the Chinese when Kublai Khan conquered Nanchao, and it was absorbed into the Mongol Empire.

Well before this event, some of the tribes had emigrated southward from Nanchao into the hills of northern Burma, north Thailand and Laos and thus established the Shan, Thai and Lao branches of the race. Such migrations were a part of the southward movement of peoples into the Indochinese peninsula, a gradual penetration by small groups drifting almost imperceptibly into the area. The early Thai kingdom of Chiengsen, for example, was founded in 773. It was the forerunner of the kingdom of Lannathai, established by King Mengrai (ruled 1259-1317) with his capital at Chiang Mai.

Other Thais moved into what was Khmer territory beginning around 700 A.D. They founded several city-states, and in 1238 two Thai chiefs gained control over Sukhothai, the Khmer capital in the north. By the end of the century, Sukhothai had become the first great center of power and civilization of the Thai people within the boundaries of the present Kingdom of Thailand. If it may be said that the political genesis of the Siamese kingdom dates from the founding of Ayutthaya, then it is equally true that the first center of Siamese culture and civilization came into being with the founding of the Sukhothai kingdom.

Phra Ruang, crowned as King Sri Intaratitya, was the first ruler of Sukhothai. One of his sons, King Ramkhaeng, ascended the throne in 1275 and brought the kingdom to the heights of its power. It extended from present-day Laos to the Andaman Sea in the west, to the Gulf in the south and into the Malay peninsula. He encouraged the spread of Buddhism in his realm, expanded and enhanced the beauty of his capital, twice visited Peking from which he brought potters who created the much-prized Sawankaloke pottery and, not least of all, gave his subjects a written script drawn from Khmer, Mon and Sanskrit sources. Some of the great works of Thai sculpture date from this Sukhothai period, especially the cast bronze Buddhas, many of which survive today.

For whatever reason, Sukhothai did not long survive after the death of this great king. Neighboring princes took various pieces of territory, and the kingdom itself became subject to Ayutthaya in the south and in a few more years disappeared entirely.

In the mid-14th century a prince of Utong, Rama Tibodi, captured Chanthaburi and Lopburi from the Khmers and established a new capital at Ayutthaya. The next great era in Thai history carries the name of this city, founded by King Rama Tibodi in 1350. Thirty-three kings ruled from this capital over a period of 417 years, and the city survived until its conquest and destruction by the Burmese in 1767. From its founding the kingdom grew rapidly by the acquisition of several neighboring Thai states. For years Ayutthaya warred on the northern kingdom of Chiang Mai and on the Khmers in Cambodia from whom the capital of Angkor was taken.

It was to the great city of Ayutthaya, in its day larger and more impressive than London, that the earliest Europeans came in the 16th century. There were traders, missionaries and mercenaries among their number. First to come were the Portuguese, who sent Duarte Fernandez in 1511, then the Spanish. Treaties were entered into with both nations. The Dutch, English and French followed, and their traders and envoys were made welcome. This initial penetration of Siam by the West was sufficient to establish the reputation of the country as the most important kingdom in all of Southeast Asia.

Notable among the early kings was King Boroma Trailokanat, whose long rule began in 1448. He centralized the government of the kingdom, reformed the laws and court ceremonies.

In 1568 the first of a number of wars with Burma occurred. The Burmese besieged Ayutthaya and after several months took the city. They were in control for a period of 15 years. In 1584 the famous warrior prince, Naresuan, organized an army of resistance against the Burmese, retook the city, fought back several new Burmese invasions and, upon the death of his father (the vassal king), ascended the throne. It was in 1592, in repelling a further Burmese attack, that King Naresuan engaged the Burmese crown prince, Min Chit Swa, in single combat, vanquished him, and the Siamese forces gained an important victory over the invaders. So thoroughly were the Burmese defeated that they were entirely expelled from the country and some Burmese territory taken, including a port area in the west. In the next year the Siamese invaded Cambodia and reduced it to the status of a vassal state. The great warrior king finally died in 1605 while campaigning against Burma in the west.

There followed a period of greater contact with the West and increased trade. With the Siamese in possession of Mergui, a port on the Bay of Bengal which had been taken by Naresuan from the Burmese, traders could now transport goods from the Indian Ocean to the China Sea without the long voyage around the Malay peninsula, by taking an overland route. Ayutthaya served as a crossroad for some of this trade. Trade prospered and the city witnessed the arrival of more traders, missionaries and others from Spain, England, France and the Netherlands.

It was in the time of King Narai, in 1664, that the Dutch threatened armed force, if necessary, to secure Siamese acceptance of a treaty which gave the Dutch East India Company certain monopoly rights in trade and extraterritorial rights for Dutch citizens in Siam. In his effort to contain the Dutch, King Narai sought some tie with one of the other great powers which might serve to counterbalance the Dutch threat.

Here begins the fascinating story of one Constantine Phaulkon — Greek adventurer extraordinary. Phaulkon, a one-time ship's cabin boy who had made his way to England and learned the language, came to the kingdom in the 1670's as a clerk or assistant to an English trader, George White, who was trading on his own in the region. In some manner, the details are not clear, he became advisor to a high treasury official in the government and later advisor to King Narai himself. At this time the government was concerned that the Dutch and Mohammedan trading interests might combine in an effort to take over Siam much in the manner they had earlier taken over Indonesia. The king is said to have solicited the aid of White and Phaulkon to see if the East India Company would take such a position in the country as to discourage the Dutch in their designs. The British apparently did not take much interest in expanding their operations, and Phaulkon decided that if the British could not be used as a counterweight to the threat, then perhaps their major rivals, the French, could. He dispatched envoys to the court of Louis XIV and at home removed a number of Mohammedan officials and otherwise sought to counter the influence of the Dutch and Moham- medans. The French were receptive to intervention in Siam, but before their own embassy could reach Ayutthaya, several members of the court organized a revolution which resulted in the overthrow of Phaulkon, who at the time possessed the powers of prime min- ister. The reason for the revolution was most likely the jealousy of the courtiers who felt Phaulkon had usurped a position that right-fully belonged to them, and he was also suspected of conspiring with the French to take over the kingdom for himself.

At about this time (1688), King Narai was incapacitated with illness, and the regent, Phra Petraja, was leader of the anti-French faction at court. He had King Narai's adopted son and heir killed, and Phaulkon was arrested, imprisoned and then executed. When Narai died, Petraja took the throne. He expelled all foreigners, except for some missionaries, and for the next 150 years the country was isolated from the west.

The next major event in Siamese history was the renewal of the wars with Burma. The Burmese advanced on Ayutthaya and besieged the city in 1760. This first siege was unsuccessful, but it was later renewed and the Burmese took the city in 1767. Ayutthaya fell! Palaces, temples, houses, everything was levelled. The king was lost. Thousands were taken captive to Burma along with cartloads of plunder. Archives and the historical records all perished in flames. The once great metropolis was literally destroyed.

A general of the Siamese forces, Phya Takh Sin, escaped from the scene of the defeat and with several hundred followers fled to the eastern shore of the Gulf of Siam. Others joined him and in a few months, at the head of several thousand fighting men, he moved up the Chao Phraya River to take Thonburi. He proclaimed himself king and began the task of reuniting the country, which by this time had broken up into several individual small states. Within a few years he had assaulted the Burmese, gained a victory, and expelled them from the country so that Thai rule was again established. In succeeding years he not only reunified the country, but repelled several Burmese invasions and subjugated Chiang Mai, Cambodia and two Laotian principalities. King Takh Sin, however, did not live to enjoy the fruits of his labors. He finally became insane and his ministers, one assumes with reluctance because of his service to the Thai people, had him killed.

He was succeeded by one of his officers, Chao Phraya Chakri (Yodfah Chulaloke), founder of the present dynasty, who was made king in 1782 as Rama I. It was he who built the Grand Palace and the Royal Chapel (Temple of the Emerald Buddha), after moving the capital from Thonburi across the river to Bangkok.

During his reign there were continuing conflicts with the Burmese and varied involvements in Cambodia, Vietnam and in the south on the peninsula. By the time of his death, in 1809, Siam had again become a powerful state. In addition to his military prowess, he was a capable administrator. Among other accomplishments he created a code of laws, known as the "Law of the Three Seals," and he reformed the Buddhist priesthood as well as bringing about a revision of the *Tripitaka*, the holy scripture of Buddhism.

Phra Buddha Lert-Lah succeeded his father as king to become Rama II in 1809, and he ruled until 1824. Early in his reign the Burmese made another attempt to invade Thailand, but this was the last real effort they made to enforce their pretensions of suzerainty over Thailand. Thereafter the threat from Burma receded.

King Lert-Lah's reign is notable for the reopening of relations with the British. This came about as the result of a conflict in British and Siamese interests in the Sultanate of Kedah on the peninsula. The Sultan of Kedah had leased Penang to the English in 1786 and later, in 1791, was forced to cede the island to them. In 1800, pirates from the mainland attacked Penang and were interfering with the food supply to the island. The British believed that the Sultan had a hand in these happenings and accordingly required him to cede the land on the mainland opposite Penang Island, called Province Wellesley, to them.

The Siamese had claimed suzerainty over Kedah since the time of the Sukhothai King Ramkhaeng in the 13th century. Their interference in the affairs of the sultanate varied with their involvement in other directions, but when the Kedah sultan was suspected of supporting the Burmese in a threatened move against Siam, King Lert-Lah sent the Governor of Nakhon Si Thammarat with an army to invade Kedah. The Sultan fled to the British (1822). The King installed a new sultan of his own choosing, and British trade with the mainland came to a standstill.

The next year the East India Company sent John Crawfurd to Bangkok to negotiate a commercial treaty. He did not get the concessions he sought, but an indirect result of his mission was the reopening of trade with the English. It remained for a subsequent mission, headed by Henry Burney in the reign of the next king, to end Siamese aspirations in western Malaya.

King Lert-Lah sought to encourage trade with foreign countries, and he is especially remembered for the extensive cultural revival that he initiated. He encouraged the arts and literature in all their forms: sculpture, the casting of Buddha images, painting, niello work, music, the dramatic arts, poetry and plays. He also was concerned with the building of new temples. He established Wat Po, continued the work started by his father at Wat Arun, and added to the Grand Palace. His endeavors were especially significant since so much of Siamese art and literature had perished in the sack of Ayutthaya by the Burmese.

When Rama II died in 1824, he had two sons by his queen. The eldest was Prince Mongkut, who was 20 at the time. It was another son, one by a minor wife, who was elected by the nobles to succeed his father inasmuch as he was older and more experienced in affairs of state. This was King Nang Klao, who became Rama III and ruled until 1851.

His reign was marked by two major conflicts. The first involved the suppression of a revolt by the Kingdom of Vientiane. The Laos had long been under the Thai rulers, and now, under the mistaken impression that the British were about to invade Siam, the Lao ruler in Vientiane made a bid for independence. After initial reverses, the Thai army defeated the Lao forces, destroyed the capital of Vientiane, and captured the insurgent prince who was then brought to Bangkok where he later died in captivity.

A second campaign was launched by the King against the Vietnamese, who had covertly supported the Vientiane rebellion, and were now interfering with Siamese supremacy in Cambodia. This second struggle was less successful, and in 1845 the Thais finally had to agree to a compromise by which Cambodia came under the joint protection of Thailand and Vietnam.

Rama III was the last of the Siamese monarchs who sought to avoid all Western influences. Even so, it was during his reign, in 1833, that a treaty of commerce and friendship was entered into by the United States and Siam. When he died, in 1851, it was his half-brother, Prince Mongkut, who succeeded him as Rama IV.

King Mongkut is known to many Americans because of Margaret Landon's novel *Anna and the King of Siam*, and its motion picture dramatization. The historical "Anna" (Mrs. Anna H. Leonowens) was an English woman brought out to the court as a teacher of English language and manners to the heir apparent, Chulalongkorn, and other children of the king. Mongkut was anything but the whimsical autocrat portrayed in the film. The film is not exhibited in Thailand and is regarded as most disrespectful. This is understandable in view of the traditional veneration with which the Thais regard their rulers.

As a matter of fact, King Mongkut is one of the most revered monarchs in Thai history. He spent 27 years as a Buddhist monk during the reign of his half-brother. He was a devout man, and at the same time had a keen and inquiring mind. He learned English from American missionary friends, and studied Pali, Sanskrit, Cambodian, Mon and Singhalese as well. He had a grasp of the history of the West, science, mathematics, Latin and astronomy. The latter was a subject of special interest to him.

While Mongkut was known for his toleration of other religions, he insisted upon discipline within the Buddhist faith. He reformed its rites and practices so that they more nearly conformed to the teachings and practices of the Lord Buddha. When monks failed to adhere to their vows or were lax in discipline he had them defrocked, and on one occasion, at least, sent them out to cut grass for the royal elephants.

The King was a most generous man. Manich Jumsai records several examples of his generosity, among them the present of $1,000 to the poor widow of an American missionary friend of his days as a monk. There was also the matter of his repeated aid to the British Consul. It seems that the Consulate was not always in funds and often faced long delays in getting money out of London for the needs of the office. When the Consul desired to acquire land upon which to build a proper consulate, and had no money available for the purpose, the King bought the necessary land and gave it to the Consul. When the time came to start construction of the buildings, the Consul was again without the necessary funds, and the King obliged with a loan. It is reported, as well, that on a further occasion the Consul had no funds with which to pay his staff, and once again Mongkut dipped into his treasury! A further, and somewhat amusing, example of his generosity is his offer of Siamese war elephants to the American president to be used in putting down the rebellion during the Civil War. The offer was actually made to President Buchanan, but by the time the letter reached Washington, Lincoln was president.

Mongkut pursued a policy of rapprochement with the West. In 1855 he entered into a commercial treaty with Great Britain, and similar treaties with other nations followed, including one with the

United States of America in 1856. He brought in numerous foreign advisors to assist in reorganizing the administration of the country and improved communications. Bangkok was linked with Burma and Penang by telegraph. Canals were dug from the city to outlying towns and areas, and he ordered the construction of the first road from the Grand Palace. This was New Road (Chalerm Krung), now one of the busiest thoroughfares in the capital. The impetus toward modernization of the kingdom had its beginning in Mongkut's reign.

The innovations that this enlightened monarch brought about during the years of his rule are legion. He created a new system of coinage and issued currency notes for the first time, installed a printing press in the Grand Palace and even provided for a court newspaper, reorganized the police service, standardized weights and measures, prohibited the use of opium, and reformed various laws and taxes.

In foreign affairs there were some setbacks. While it is true that the several treaties of friendship and commerce and the embassies that were sent abroad resulted in an increase in trade, and brought the country out of isolation and into contact with other nations of the world, it was during this period that the extension of Siamese control over Trengganu and Pahang in Malaya was effectively halted by the British. The latter, willingly or not, were soon to assume a more active role in the Malay peninsula, in some measure at the expense of traditional Thai influence.

A more serious development was the French takeover of Chochin China and the establishment of a French protectorate over Cambodia. Here the Siamese were faced with a fait accompli. A French admiral sailed up the Mekhong River and forced King Narodom of Cambodia to sign a treaty providing for French "protection" of his land. Narodom complained to Mongkut, since Cambodia had theretofore been under the Siamese, and Mongkut protested to the French government in Paris. Ultimately Mongkut had no choice but to ratify the treaty (1867), though he did secure French recognition of the Siamese claim to the provinces of Battambang and Siem Reap, which were a part of the old Cambodia.

The King's death, in 1868, was indirectly the result of his natural curiosity concerning things scientific. He had calculated the time of a total eclipse of the sun and had invited a number of foreign dignitaries, consuls and the Governor of Singapore to come to Wah-Kor, from which place the eclipse was best to be observed. The

King himself had supervised the preparation of lodgings for his guests and the court deep in the jungle at Wah-Kor. Unfortunately, the area was full of malaria, and he contracted the fever from which he died soon after his return to Bangkok.

Chulalongkorn succeeded his father on the throne as Rama V. He was but fifteen years old when his father died, and spent the next five years in a monastery prior to assuming the rule. During this period the country was governed by a regent. Chulalongkorn visited India, Java, Burma, Malaya and Singapore prior to assuming control of the government when he became of age in 1873. He was thus a much-traveled monarch, in comparison with his predecessors. His long reign spanned a period of 42 years, from 1868 until 1910. It was a time of great change in the world and an era of colonialism, when both France and Great Britain were expanding their territories in Southeast Asia. Chulalongkorn ably continued the work of his father in bringing about the modernization of the country, and his internal reforms and programs of change affected virtually every aspect of national life.

Immediately upon taking control of the government he instituted a Council of State and a Privy Council to serve as advisory bodies. He installed modern administration methods and changed the system of administration to bring about greater centralization of authority. Village headmen were made responsible to the leaders of cantons (groups of villages). Leaders of cantons were responsible to district chiefs, who were in turn responsible to the governors of provinces. Provincial governors were made dependent on the central administration, and appointments to the office of governor, formerly hereditary, were in future to be based on merit. Various ministries were created for war, finance, justice, agriculture and other departments, to improve the administration of government. The practice of farming out the collection of taxes to private individuals, as tax collectors, was abolished, and a Revenue Department was established for the payment of taxes direct to the government.

In the area of national defense the army and navy were modernized, and training schools instituted for military cadets and the navy. A Royal Survey Department was created to map the seas for navigation and to prepare maps which could be used in defending the country from attack.

The communications network was rapidly expanded. New canals were dug, roads constructed, and in the 1890's the building of a railroad was commenced. In 1881 the first telephones came into use.

Substantial advances in public health and education were made. A Public Health Department was established, a medical school and a school for nurses opened, and facilities organized for the preparation of vaccines and medicines. The King founded several schools, Buddhist colleges and a teacher training school. A Ministry of Education was introduced. The school for the royal pages, in the course of time, grew into a School for Civil Servants and from the latter Chulalongkorn University eventually evolved.

Numerous measures were taken to develop the economy and natural resources. An Irrigation Department was given the task of cutting irrigation canals to aid in growing rice. A Mining Department supervised mineral resources and mining, and the teak forests were placed under a Forestry Department. Rice culture—then and now so important to the Thai economy—was given special attention. Seeds produced at government model farms were distributed to farmers to improve the quality of the rice and crop yields, and the general improvement of rice-farming methods was encouraged.

King Chulalongkorn was also active in encouraging Thai arts and culture. He founded a museum, a national library and had a printed edition of the *Tripitaka* prepared in the Thai language. During his reign several outstanding examples of Thai architecture were constructed, among them Wat Benchamaborpit (the Marble Temple), Chakri Palace and the Throne Hall (now National Assembly Hall).

However occupied he must have been with the internal affairs of his kingdom, the King found time for a visit to India and for two grand tours of Europe. He visited most of the European countries and passed through Egypt as well.

His crowning achievement and greatest contribution to his kingdom was no less than preserving its very existence and independence as a sovereign state in a period of colonialism during which neighboring states, one after another, came under the denomination of the British or the French. France, in particular, coveted Siamese territory.

The intricacies of Siamese foreign policy during the period need not be traced in detail. In brief outline, a chain of events commenced with French seizure of Saigon in 1859. With the gradual addition of Vietnamese territory over the next two decades, France had annexed the entire country by 1883. Further French conquest of Tongking prompted the Siamese to strengthen their hold on neighboring Laos, which had been subject to the Thai kingdom for more than a century. The French claimed Laos on grounds that the country had formerly paid tribute to Vietnam, and since Vietnam now belonged to France, Laos was accordingly a French possession. At the very least the French insisted on control of all of the territory east of the Mekong River. Whatever the merit of such claims, and of others which were advanced, the French backed their position with military force. A climax was reached when two French gunboats blasted their way up the river to Bangkok. The French Minister presented the Royal Government with an ultimatum demanding that Siam give up all that area to the left bank of the Mekong, pay a large sum in reparations to the French and make a reply to French demands within 48 hours. Other demands were subsequently made, and the Gulf of Siam was declared to be under blockade by the French navy.

It is more than just possible that the French sought to precipitate a conflict which would enable them to take over the rich Chao Phraya River valley, the very heartland of Siam. The British, perhaps envious of the success of French colonization in Southeast Asia, were prompted by these events to strengthen their own position by annexing upper Burma. While they were willing to lend their moral support to the Siamese in their troubles with the French, they would go no further. This intangible support was not a very useful weapon with which to oppose French columns in the eastern border areas or the French navy in the south, and the Thais had to accept French terms. A treaty was concluded. Several years later the Thais had to cede the provinces of Battambang and Siemreap to the French to secure the withdrawal of French troops from their country.

Near the close of the reign, in 1909, Siam relinquished to the British all claims and rights over the Malay states of Kelantan, Trengganu, Kedah and Perlis. In return the British gave up their extraterritorial rights in Siam and provided the Siamese with a large loan for the construction of a railroad.

Chulalongkorn's foreign policy resulted in the loss of some territorial rights, but this was a small price to pay for the survival of the nation. His long reign came to an end with his death in 1910. His rule seems closely linked with the present day—his grandson, the popular Bhumibol, now sits on the throne.

Upon the death of his father, Crown Prince Vajiravudh ascended the throne as Rama VI. He had been educated in England at Oxford and attended Sandhurst. During his reign a system of compulsory education was instituted by the Education Act of 1921, and he provided a substantial endowment of land from crown properties for Chulalongkorn University when it was founded. He possessed a considerable talent as a literary man, and in addition to the original works that he wrote he translated several of Shakespeare's plays into the Thai language.

Vajiravudh brought Thailand into the First World War on the side of the Allies, and subsequently the country became a member of the League of Nations. During his rule there was a notable growth in nationalistic feeling in Siam. Regrettably he was not successful in keeping the budget in balance, and national finances were in a rather bad way when his successor came to the throne. Since the king had no male offspring at the time of his death, his younger brother succeeded him.

The new ruler, King Prajadhipok, ascended the throne as Rama VII in 1925 and ruled until his abdication in 1934. He was faced with an exhausted treasury, and the worldwide depression of the 1930's hampered the efforts of his government to restore fiscal responsibility.

He was the last of the absolute monarchs in the Kingdom of Siam. In 1932, a bloodless coup overthrew the absolute monarchy and brought about government under a constitution. The motivation for the coup and the establishment of a constitutional monarchy was to be found in the widely held belief among students and young intellectuals that absolutism was outmoded and that Siam should have a constitution as so many other modern nations had. Among the student groups abroad there was, in particular, a group of students in France especially concerned to bring this about. Among their number were Pibul Songgram and Pridi Panomyong, the former a son of a wealthy Chinese merchant and Thai mother, and the latter the son of a minor Siamese government official. These two were to provide the coup leadership and for years thereafter were active in government on the highest level.

An opportunity for the coup was soon presented. As a result of the severe world economic depression and as a measure of internal economy, numerous senior officials had been let out of the government and the pay of other government employees reduced. The promoters of the coup, who now called the movement the "People's Party," allied themselves with some of these recently relieved officials, both military and civilian, and quickly enlisted the support of younger members of government who had been educated abroad and who were imbued with the conviction that the common people were entitled to a greater share in government.

In June (1932), the leaders of the coup seized the government, arrested several senior princes and nobles, including the chief of police, and served the king with an ultimatum calling for a constitution. The king himself was not opposed to a constitutional regime for his country and consented to cooperate with the coup leaders and their People's Party.

The People's Party then inaugurated a coup government with a former Supreme Court Judge as prime minister. During this period, Pridi served as a sort of chief administrator. Pibul handled the military, and a third in this triumvirate of strong men was Colonel Phya Bahol Pholpayuhasena. The party also appointed a committee to draft a permanent constitution, which was duly submitted to the king and promulgated toward the end of the year. Under the new constitution a unicameral national assembly of 156 representatives was established, half elected by the people and half appointed by the government. A cabinet was created to exercise the executive power.

A word about the coup d'etat in Thailand as a means of changing governments is in order at this point. There have been some 30 such coups since this original one in 1932 up to the 1973 student riots and expulsion of Kittikachorn. New constitutions have followed coups with considerable regularity (ten so far, and an eleventh has now been drafted as this book is being written). Fortunately most of the coups have been bloodless, and the stability of the Crown has tended to offset their disruptive nature and lend an aura of permanence to governmental institutions.

Soon after the new government was organized, Pridi presented an elaborate economic plan that would have placed land ownership in the hands of the government and made government employees of the farmers. The plan was widely regarded as communistic and it was rejected. Pridi himself, though later investigated and cleared of the charge, was accused of being a Communist. He left the government and went to Europe.

The king and the conservatives were soon at loggerheads with the liberal government over policy. The government survived a royalist revolt led by Prince Bovaradej in 1933, and in the following year the king went to England for medical treatment. It is said that he felt that his own training and experience as an absolute ruler ill-fitted him to nurture the growth of constitutional government and that he should therefore make way for a successor who would not be thus handicapped. He accordingly abdicated in 1934 and remained abroad until his death in 1941.

At the time of his abdication King Prajadhipok had not designated a successor. A Council of Regency selected the child of his younger brother as the new ruler. This was Ananda Mahidol, who ascended the throne as Rama VIII. He was a child of ten at the time, a student at Lausanne in Switzerland, and a regency governed during his minority. Colonel Phya Bahol served as prime minister until the end of 1938 and was succeeded in office by Pibul Songgram.

This young army colonel, one of the original promoters of the 1932 coup, headed the government of Thailand when the Japanese entered World War II with the attack on Pearl Harbor in 1941. It was officially *Thailand* now, not *Siam*. The notion of a "greater Thailand," one that might one day include some of the peoples of Laos, the Shan states and even south China, who shared the Thai language and culture, had gained currency in the late 1930's. This concept was at the basis of the change in the name of the country from Siam to Thailand (which literally means "land of the free") in 1939. A practical extension of territory occurred in 1940 when, after negotiations in Tokyo with the French Vichy government, the Thais regained two Cambodian and two Laotian provinces that had been ceded to French Indochina during Chulalongkorn's reign. (These areas were restored to France at the end of the war, however.)

In December 1941 the Japanese demanded permission from the Thai government to enter and pass through the country in their drive on Burma and Malaya. Pridi, now back in the country and serving as a regent for the boy-king, advised resistance. Pibul, however, was faced with a powerful armed nation on his doorstep and was aware that he could expect no aid from the British in Malaya and Singapore. He granted the requested permission. The Japanese promptly occupied the country and moved troops into Malaya and Burma across

Thai territory. On the surface, at least, the Thai government collaborated with the Japanese while at the same time other Thais provided valuable underground aid to the West.

After the fall of Singapore and Axis victories in North Africa and on the Eastern European Front, Pibul bowed to Japanese pressure — for as it then appeared, Japan and the Axis might well be victorious in the war — and declared war on the United States and Great Britain. Thailand incidentally received four Malaysian provinces from the Japanese, perhaps as a sort of "thank you." They were relinquished at the end of the war.

Whatever alternative course of action Pibul might have had, and perhaps he had none, many Thais opposed his war-time policy. The Thai minister in Washington, for example, refused to deliver his government's declaration of war on the U.S. on the grounds that it did not represent the will of the Thai people. The same minister, M. R. Seni Pramjoy, organized a "Free Thai" movement among Thai students attending American colleges and universities. Pridi launched a "Free Thai" movement within Thailand itself and worked with U.S. and British intelligence in organizing a resistance and in supplying information to the Southeast Asia Command in Ceylon. Popular support of Pibul's government ebbed as it became increasingly apparent that the Japanese would be defeated, and in 1944 he resigned. His successor, Nai Khuang Aphaiwongse, covertly welcomed U.S. and British personnel and supplies to reinforce interior forces who were hopeful of making a strike against the Japanese. Then came the end of the war and Japanese surrender.

Seni Pramjoy, returning from the United States, then became prime minister. His government promptly declared the 1942 declaration of war against the U.S. and Great Britain null and void. Because the U.S. had not recognized the declaration in the first place, this conciliatory act of the Thai government was merely acknowledged and accepted. The British, however, had regarded the war declaration as an act of belligerency and peace treaties were therefore entered into with both Britain and France. Great Britain demanded, among other things, delivery from the Thais of one and one-half million tons of rice. The French required repossession of the territories returned to Thailand early in the war as the price of supporting the Thai bid for membership in the United Nations.

Pridi and his supporters dominated the postwar political scene in Thailand. His government was plagued with all of the problems of this difficult period. Then came the untimely and mysterious death of the youthful King Ananda Mahidol.

The events of this tragedy have been amply recorded but the mystery never solved. The king had returned to Thailand from his studies in Switzerland late in 1945. His mother and younger brother, the present king, accompanied him. He had planned to return to Switzerland in mid-June 1946. A few days before his planned departure, early on the morning of June 9, he was found dead in his bed, a bullet through his forehead.

The theory of accidental death has been widely accepted. The king was known to have had interest in revolvers and shooting. It was theorized from the circumstances that the weapon had discharged accidentally while he was handling it. The nature of the wound and other circumstances seem to have ruled out suicide. On the other hand there are many who believe that the king was murdered for political reasons. Whatever the truth of the matter, his demise is still the subject of conjecture. Pridi's government does not appear to have investigated with the alacrity that might have been expected. When he resigned nothing seems to have been done by the successor government of Luang Thamrong Nawasawat. Whatever findings the next government and later governments might have made, they have not clearly resolved the mystery.

When King Ananda died, his brother, Bhumibol Adulyadej the present king, succeeded him as Rama IX. Bhumibol was born on December 5, 1927 in the United States at Cambridge, Massachusetts, where his father was at the time a medical student at Harvard. When his brother died, the present king was 18 years old and pursuing his education in Switzerland. He completed his studies abroad and returned to Bangkok in 1950. Very soon after his return he was married to the lovely Sirikit, and the coronation took place in May of that year. The royal couple have four children: Crown Prince Vajiralongkorn (born July 28, 1952), and the Princesses Ubol Ratana, Sirindhorn and Chulabhorn.

Bhumibol is the symbol of national unity, and his popularity amongst the Thais is unbounded. He is a "working" king and with Queen Sirikit travels even into the most remote areas of the country in discharging the tasks of his kingship. As a constitutional monarch he possesses little actual political power. He is nominal head of state, supreme commander of the armed forces and head of the church, but he rules only through his government.

Soon after Bhumibol's succession to the throne, the military under the leadership of General Sarit Thanarat, chief of the army, and General Phao Sriyanon, chief of the police, overthrew the government. Pridi fled to exile in Red China. The coup leaders installed Pibul Songgram as prime minister, and he continued at the head of government until another coup in 1957 brought Field Marshal Sarit to power. In this interim the triumvirate, Pibul, Sarit and Phao, dominated government.

Pibul was a man of strong will. He had been head of government during the war period, and now sought to make Thailand strong in time of peace. One of his major achievements was the construction of a network of roads to link up the provinces with the capital. This greatly aided the development of the more remote areas. Land could be cultivated more profitably when produce could be gotten to market. He also encouraged industry and organized the Tobacco Monopoly and factories for the production of cement, paper and gunnysacks. After a trip abroad in 1955, where he observed democracy in action, Pibul made loud protestations of the need for democracy in Thailand and for parliamentary government. For a time after his return he somewhat relaxed controls on freedom of public expression.

On the negative side, under Pibul corruption in government reached new highs. There was extensive embezzlement, and some of the misapplication of funds in the government's own projects and undertakings bordered on the ludicrous. He maintained his personal power largely by playing off Phao and the police against Sarit and the army. Phao was Director General of Police during Pibul's rule (1948-1957) and was made Minister of Interior in 1957. He was ruthless and corrupt. His own police were involved in a vast network of illegal opium smuggling and sale. In fact, opium was virtually a police monopoly.

The 1957 coup that finally toppled Pibul from power, grew out of a test of strength between Sarit, as commander-in-chief of the Thai army, and Police General Phao. Army and police were about equal in strength and armament. Irregularities in the elections of February 1957, which were blatantly permitted by the police (some said as a forerunner of Phao's intention to take over the government himself), set the stage. Illegal ballots were used. Votes were purchased wholesale, voters' lists were disregarded in some areas and ballot boxes were stuffed by individuals who had no right to vote. Soon after Phao was made Minister of Interior, Pibul was warned by the Sarit faction to remove Phao, or else! Pibul declined and Marshal Sarit took over the government by coup. Pibul fled posthaste to Japan and there later died. Phao made his way to Switzerland, some said in order to be closer to his bank accounts, where he died in 1960.

The significance of Sarit's revolution was that it aimed at national development rather than the aggrandisement of the man at the top. He installed an interim government with General Thanom Kittikachorn as prime minister, and then went abroad to secure needed medical treatment. He returned from Great Britain and the United States, where he had surgery, in October 1958 and launched the revolution as leader of the Revolutionary Party. He removed his deputy, Thanom, as head of government and became the one-man ruler of the country. Thanom and General Prapat Charusathien were later to serve as Sarit's deputies. The constitution was discarded, the Assembly dissolved, political parties disbanded and martial law declared.

From the point of view of the western democracies, dictatorship, whether of the right or the left, is generally held to be bad. Sarit was certainly an authoritarian ruler. However, any objective appraisal of his regime must credit his government with genuine accomplishments which were of major benefit to the nation. Pibul's government had run up a vast debt, and Sarit straightened out the national finances. His ministers were more honest and efficient than their predecessors. He moved vigorously against the Communists, cleaned up the police service, acted to control the narcotic drug trade and implemented a plan for economic development. Compulsory primary education was increased from four to seven years. In short, substantial economic and social advances were made during the period that he was head of state. When Sarit died at the end of 1963, his deputy, General Thanom Kittikachorn, became prime minister.

In the years following World War II, and continuing to the present time, Thailand has been active in seeking to prevent the spread of Communism in Southeast Asia. This has involved close cooperation with the member states of SEATO and an especially close relation with the United States. During the period of the Vietnam war, the United States maintained several air bases within Thailand from which bombing missions were flown against the enemy in both North and South Vietnam. At the end of the war, when the U.S. began to reduce the number of air personnel in Thailand, the Thai government expressed the fear that such reductions could result in increased Communist activity in the region. On the other hand, some intensely nationalistic student activist groups have more recently loudly urged the withdrawal of all U.S. bases.

From 1932 on, the Communist Party in Thailand has been illegal, with the exception of one or two brief periods. Communistic activity has been rigorously suppressed. At times the government, in its own interest and for its own purposes, may have blown up the Communist "threat," and from time to time Communist subversion has been blamed for events with which the party and its supporters possibly had no actual connection. Fighting the Communist menace – in fact or fancy – has been one means used to justify the strongly authoritarian governments which have held power.

This is not to say that there is no Communist threat in Thailand. Thailand has four Communist parties – Thai, Chinese, Vietnamese and Malayan – and they are all illegal. So far as political power is concerned, they have none. Nor have the Communists been able to surface in an overt role in politics. But they have played and may still be playing a role within the country. Communist efforts have been focused on the press and on the overseas Chinese. The Communists have sought to buy both the Thai and Chinese press by bribery and payments, in order to insinuate their ideology. How effective these efforts have been is very much open to question.

Until 1958 Thailand bought from mainland China and among the imports were publications and books as well as Chinese-produced motion pictures. Obviously these items influenced the thinking of those who were open to influence. This is particularly true of the usually well-concealed propaganda and ideological teachings in the motion pictures which were widely viewed by the Chinese in Thailand. In 1958 Field Marshal Sarit banned all such imports.

Communist agents were also active in the field of education, primarily among the Chinese. They often organized study groups, outside the regular education system, which were designed to spread the Communist ideology, and circulated textbooks which reflected the party line. There is also the problem of Chinese students who have pursued their higher education in the Chinese language. They have taken advanced training at mainland Chinese universities and colleges. After completing their courses of study, some have returned to Thailand surreptitiously as Red agents.

The Thai government has firmly opposed these activities and in this it has had the support of the U.S. In addition, in order to combat the effectiveness of Communist propaganda and to show the Thais that America is a friendly and staunch ally, the U.S. government has spent millions and millions of dollars on various projects in Thailand in the economic, educational, agricultural, health and other fields. American tax dollars went into the construction of "Friendship Road," which has improved communications throughout the central plain and into the northeast of the country, and various other projects. Regrettably, as has been the case elsewhere, American public relations have been so low key that most of the Thais are unaware of this aid which, while it is certainly benefiting the recipients, has not much improved the American image as it might well have. Actually U.S. aid to Thailand has been much less than has been spent elsewhere to less purpose. Basically the American view has been that by extending aid to Thailand that country is strengthened and accordingly Communist expansionism is in like measure discouraged.

The direct impact that Communism has on Thailand has taken the form of irregular guerrilla activity in the northeast. There is Communist infiltration in this area along the border with Laos. Thai-born Chinese, some of them undoubtedly trained in guerrilla operations inside China or in North Vietnam, cross the Mekong River on the border and carry on subversive activities. They have been responsible for the killing of many social workers, teachers and others in this area. The government is acutely aware of the problem and strives continuously to combat it, but the border is long and rooting out these subversives is a difficult task. Best estimates are that in late 1974 there are as many as 7,000 insurgents in the northeast along the Laos border area.

In the belief that the problem of Communism in the northeast has an economic base, strong efforts are being made to improve conditions in the villages in this area. Public health measures, a better diet, the introduction of new crops and the roads to enable the farmer to get them to market — these and other steps to improve the economy and bring about social betterment seem best calculated to remove the conditions which have nurtured Communist success elsewhere.

There has also been a problem, now and again, with Communist guerrillas and bandits on the Malayan border to the south. Here the Thai and Malaysian governments have cooperated closely to minimize such disturbances.

Short of an armed Communist assault so massive as to inundate the nation's defensive capabilities, there is every reason to believe that the Thais are quite capable of containing and eventually eradicating the Red insurgency that has been so troublesome since the early 1950's. Perhaps most potent of all defenses, whether against the colonialism of past centuries or the infiltration of the Reds along the northeast border, is the proud spirit of independence innate in the Thai character. They ever seek to be masters of their own destiny.

As noted above, General Thanom Kittikachorn became head of the government on Sarit's death in 1963. His government supported U.S. policy in South Vietnam, and in addition to permitting American air bases within their country they sent 12,000 troops to cooperate with American forces in Vietnam. Diplomatic relations with Cambodia were broken off after Sihanouk allowed North Vietnamese troops to come into his country and receive supplies through the Cambodian port of Sihanoukville. When Lon Nol took over power in 1970, the Thai government immediately re-established diplomatic relations and gave support to the Cambodians in their struggle against the Communists.

In mid-1968 a new constitution was promulgated, unique in that it established a separation of powers between the executive and the legislature. Political parties were authorized, and national elections were held for the lower house of parliament in the next year. While the legislature now could function as an institutionalized voice of public opinion in guiding public policies, government was still very much in the hands of military and bureaucratic leaders.

It may be that the coup d'etat is going out of fashion in Thailand, for the most recent change of government took place not as the result of a coup but in consequence of an astonishing student upheaval that occurred in October 1973. Both Prime Minister Thanom and Deputy Prime Minister Prapat Charusathien were ousted and fled abroad, as did Thanom's son, Colonel Narong. The latter was accused of being the chief manipulator behind the flagrant corruption that was tolerated by the regime.

What started as a student rally grew into a demonstration of more than a hundred thousand people. When the mob got out of hand, there was the inevitable confrontation between the demonstrators and the police and military. Sporadic fighting broke out and continued for several hours during which several hundreds of persons were killed or wounded. Thanom and his supporters called for additional troops, but these were not supplied. The military tended to support the aims of the students rather than the government. Throughout the disturbances the police kept a low profile, so low in fact that student leaders had to call on the Boy Scouts to direct Bangkok's traffic. Thanom met with the king, resigned his office, and left the country.

An interim government was then formed under the leadership of Professor Sanya Dharmasakti, the rector of Thammasat University. The king himself announced, in December, the appointment of a new National Convention which subsequently met to select a National Legislative Assembly. The Assembly has the task, among others, of passing on a new constitution.

It is to be hoped that the new constitution and the new government that it will bring forth will be able to provide the more democratic way of life that the Thai people are seeking. Democracy, as practiced in the West, is still something for the future, but the trend is toward, rather than away from, a democratic form of government.

Democracy, per se, faces many problems in Thailand: a disinterested, virtually apathetic peasantry; power long concentrated in the military; all too-frequent corruption; the threat of subversion. The political system itself is relatively undeveloped. Political parties, so necessary for the functioning of a democratic system, have been banned from time to time. Elections traditionally don't arouse much public enthusiasm, and the popular vote is relatively small. Historically the country has been conditioned to accept strong authority, in times past that of the absolute monarch, then that of one or another political strong men or military leaders (e.g., Pibul, Sarit, Kittikachorn).

Such democracy as the Thais have enjoyed has been, to be sure, of an immature kind. "Western style" democracy cannot simply be decreed and hence come into being. A groundwork must first be built from the villages on up. Much of the electorate must undergo a process of education in terms of the issues involved. Popular, altruistic leadership must be developed. Distinctly Thai institutions must be created to implement representative government. Simply importing foreign models will not do. The ancient "village" democracy may suit Thai needs better than the western variety, at least for now. Some means must be found to link this type of "direct democracy" with the machinery of government on higher levels and at the top.

As a President of Pakistan has commented (*Foreign Affairs*, July 1960) concerning the essential nature of democracy if it is to function successfully in Asian lands: "It should be simple to understand, easy to work and cheap to sustain. It should put to the voter only such questions as he can answer in the light of his own personal knowledge and understanding without external prompting. It should ensure the effective participation of all citizens in the affairs of the country up to the level of their mental horizon and intellectual calibre. It should be able to produce reasonably strong and stable government."

Today Thailand is at the crossroads of Southeast Asia. It occupies a truly unique position. In many ways the country supplies a link between the Western world and the nations of Southeast Asia. It is the permanent headquarters of the Southeast Asia Treaty Organization (SEATO) and the seat of numerous regional offices of United Nations agencies, among them the World Health Organization and UNESCO. More important, Thailand reflects the culture of the region and this because of all of the countries in the area, it alone was never subject to one or another of the colonial powers. Thailand was situated between the French sphere of influence in French Indochina, Laos, Viet Nam, on the east, and the British sphere on the west and south in Burma, India and Malaysia, and became subject to neither. Thailand has thus, as an independent nation for many centuries, transmitted without dilution a cultural heritage going back for nearly a thousand years. It may well be that Thailand will fill an important role in the establishment of an Asian community. This prospect is reflected by the hospitable role which Bangkok plays in welcoming numerous international meetings, whether in the fields of science, politics or economics.

The Thais have been active in Southeast Asian regional affairs. They were instrumental in founding the Association of Southeast Asia (ASA) in 1961. This group includes Malaysia, the Philippines and Thailand. Thailand is also a member of the Association of Southeast Asian Nations (ASEAN), along with Malaysia, Singapore, Indonesia and the Philippines. The country was also a prime mover in organizing the Asia and Pacific Council (ASPAC), a nine-nation group including South Korea, Malaysia, Australia, New Zealand, Japan, Nationalist China, the Philippines, South Vietnam and the Thais. These last two groups aim at economic and cultural cooperation, to gain by cooperative action what might not be attainable by the individual states working alone in an age of superpowers.

Chapter 3

SAWADI —

A VISIT TO THAILAND

"*Sawadi*" — the universal spoken greeting, the "hello" of the Thais. The visitor will hear it often. He will also observe, almost from the first moments of his visit, the traditional Thai sign of salutation or mutual recognition that is called a "*wai*" (ไหว้) in the Thai language. It consists of raising both hands, palms and fingers joined and lightly touching the body somewhere between the upper chest and face. The higher the hands are elevated, the greater the respect shown. The person receiving the salutation responds in like manner. The "wai" is traditionally also rendered when one takes his departure. It may also be used as a polite gesture of thanks. The junior in age or rank customarily is the first to extend the salutation. Armed with a "Sawadi" and mastery of the "Wai" the *farang* (the common term for a foreigner) can scarcely go wrong in Thailand! Be that as it may, the traveler is certain to find a friendly welcome for the Thais are a friendly people and most want to be helpful.

The giant jet starts its approach to the Bangkok area well to the north over the flat central plain and the winding Chao Phraya River. In a few minutes the aircraft is on the runway at Bangkok's Don Muang Airport, some 24 kilometers from the downtown area. It is one of the most modern international airports in Southeast Asia and is equipped to accomodate even the largest of the new jets. Customs, immigration and public health services are provided on a 24-hour basis and entry and exit formalities normally take only a few minutes.

Don Muang is situated on the northern highway (Bahon Yothin Road) that runs from Bangkok to Chiang Mai in the north. Taxis are readily available for the ride into the city. There isn't exactly a standard rate, so some bargaining may be in order. This is especially the case because many Bangkok cabs don't use a meter. This is universally true if one takes a samlor, which is a three-wheeled cycle-powered cab of which there are hundreds in the city. Taxi fares are quite low as compared with those charged in other urban centers. Tipping is not required and is generally not expected, unless of course the driver has been especially helpful with luggage or some other courtesy.

Bangkok, the nation's capital, is situated on the Chao Phraya River. It was once on the Gulf, but over many, many centuries silt deposits carried into the Gulf by the river created a new land area and the city is now about 20 miles inland. The country immediately surrounding the city is a flat plain and for the most part given over to the cultivation of rice. The river is navigable by ocean-going vessels, and the New Port is about five miles south of Bangkok where ships load and unload in the customs area.

Bangkok literally means the "place where olives grow." It was once a small fishing village on the river. When Rama I moved his capital, in 1782, from Thonburi across the river to the east bank, he renamed it "Krung Thep" — City of Angels. But to Westerners, and indeed to most Thais themselves, the city is Bangkok.

Not so many years ago transport within the city was largely by a network of canals (*klongs*). While many of these still exist, a large number have been filled in to provide streets which are today literally jammed with vehicular traffic. In the last ten years the number of vehicles has quadrupled with only a small increase in the number of traffic arteries. The klongs are much used. There are still more boats than autos in this city, once dubbed the "Venice of the East." There are even a few areas which are still accessible only by klong.

New Road, the longest and oldest street and the second to be paved, was once an elephant path. It is lined with shops and runs through the business center. Petburi Road is a modern six-lane highway. Ratchadamnoen Avenue, with its Democracy Monument, is lined with office buildings and government ministries. Each of the main thoroughfares seems to have its own distinctive character. The western end of Ratchadamnoen connects with Chao Fa Road and the new Phrapinklao Bridge, across the Chao Phraya, which links

Thonburi with Bangkok. The bridge has brought added growth to Thonburi and the latter is now very much a part of the greater Bangkok area.

Shops selling a particular item tend to concentrate along certain streets. Along one street a dozen shops all sell shoes, along another the shops will offer religious articles, Buddha images, tables and stands used in worship and similar articles.

The up-river end of Bangkok is less congested and here there are numerous palaces, wats, government bureaus, monuments and offices of international organizations. It is a city of marked contrasts. Modern office buildings and luxury hotels are often not far removed from old monasteries and from areas where the poor live in rude huts much as they did a century ago. By way of further contrast, Thai classical dancers may be performing an age-old story reflecting the culture of centuries past just a few steps away from a nightclub.

The broad Chao Phraya is an integral part of city life. Here the river traffic reaches a crescendo of frenzy on a busy morning. There are great rice barges, sampans, tourist launches, water buses, junks, and the "longtails" — skiffs with outboard motors with long drive shafts.

In Bangkok the river plays an important part in the ceremony of Tod Kathin which provides the occasion for a most unusual and colorful pageant in October of each year. The ceremony is observed throughout Thailand and marks the day on which new robes are given to the monks. The pageant consists of a great procession of more than 30 royal barges which are oared down the river from a landing near the Grand Palace to the Wat Arun in Thonburi. They are long, narrow boats, painted gold and embellished with carvings and gold leaf. The oarsmen are dressed in bright red costumes and head-dresses. They row with marvelous precision, and the spectacle attracts thousands of spectators.

The king himself sits in a pavilion under a silken roof of crimson and gold on the last and largest of the barges with its great swan-head prow reared skyward. In a preceeding barge ceremonial drummers herald his approach. At the temple, His Majesty debarks, is greeted by his ministers, and then proceeds into the temple where he presents the robes and completes the religious ceremony.

At other times of year the royal barges may be viewed in a huge shed off the Chao Phraya. Several are very old. One, the king's auxiliary barge, was built during the reign of Rama I.

The many klongs in the Bangkok area, as well as the river, provide important avenues of transportation. A boat trip on one of these is a fascinating adventure. On one of the larger klongs there is an early morning floating market to which the market boats come each day. It's a noisy time. There are sampans laden with vegetables, fruits, fish, meat, soft drinks, coffee, cooking utensils, hats, and what not else. The admixture of sampans, children swimming, cargo boats, and tourists presents an ever-changing kaleidoscopic view of this aspect of Bangkok. There are floating markets in other cities as well. A boat ride on a rural klong can also be most interesting. Here one sees the rice fields, the orchards, farms, waterbuffalo, and gets a view of rural life at firsthand. Elsewhere the route may be through thick jungle of palms, huge ferns and vines with an unbelievable variety of wild orchids.

The most famous, and the oldest, landmark in Bangkok is the Grand Palace with the adjoining Royal Chapel of the Emerald Buddha (the *Wat Phra Keo*). The construction of the palace was commenced in 1782 soon after King Rama I moved the capital to its present site. Inside the great courtyard the golden roofs and spires, the gateways and stately reception halls provide the most magnificent examples of Siamese architecture to be found anywhere in the kingdom.

The earliest buildings are the two groups of residences, the Mahamontien and the Dusit-Mahaprasad. A third group, the Chakri-Mahaprasad, was constructed much later by Chulalongkorn and was used by him as a residence. The Grand Palace is no longer utilized as a royal residence, but it is used for certain state occasions and for the coronation of a new king.

The Mahamontien group consists of the Amarindra Audience Hall, Paisal Taksin Hall and the Chakrabardibiman building. Court ceremonies take place within the Audience Hall of Amarindra before a heavily gilded throne surmounted by a canopy of white cloth in nine tiers. Just behind the throne there is a large boat-shaped altar. The coronation of a monarch takes place in Paisal Hall. In the coronation chamber there is the coronation chair as well as a curious octagonal seat from which the king receives the invitation to rule from the people. The altar in the center contains the symbolic figure of Siam. The Chakrabardibiman building ad-

Wat Po (Temple of the Reclining Buddha)

Wat Benchamaborpit (Marble Temple)

National Assembly Hall

Rama V Mural, National Assembly Hall

Lacquer Pavilion, Suan Pakkad Palace

Floating Market

National Museum in Bangkok

Khon Performers

Khon Masks

Thai Classical Dancers

City Post Shrine in Bangkok

Thai Boxing

Loy Krathong (Festival of Lights)

Ploughing Ceremony (Pramane Ground)

Water Throwing Festival

Royal Summer Palace Pavilion (Bang Pa-In)

Ayutthaya

Wat Phra Tadt Doi Sutep (Chiang Mai)

Teak Forest Elephant at Work

Elephant Round-Up at Surin

Umbrella Making in Chiang Mai

Pattaya Beach

Water Throwing Festival

Bridge on the River Kwai (Kanchanaburi)

Phra Pathom Chedi

joins Paisal Hall and it was occupied as a residence by Rama I, Rama II and Rama III. Here there are a reception hall, which now contains the royal regalia, and the royal bedchamber and dressing room. Later monarchs have customarily spent a night or so here following their coronation as a gesture signifying their taking up official residence in the palace.

In the Dusit-Mahaprasad there is a mother-of-pearl throne of exquisite design, again surmounted by the nine-tiered white canopy which is the mark of a duly crowned king. The wall covering in the audience hall is of special interest. At first glance it might pass for an expensive wallpaper, but upon closer examination it will be observed to consist of a single hand-painted design that has been painstakingly duplicated several hundred times to cover the wall areas from the high ceiling almost to the richly carpeted floor.

Only the reception wings of the Chakri-Mahaprasad are ordinarily in use and these are decorated with portrait galleries. The central throne-hall, which is between the two reception wings, is the place where foreign diplomatic representatives present their credentials. In addition to the heavy crystal decorations in the hall, all gifts of reigning monarchs to King Chulalongkorn, there are several paintings of diplomatic receptions given to Siamese envoys by the courts of Louis XIV, Queen Victoria and by the Emperor Napoleon III.

The Boromabiman building, which is a bit to the east of the Mahamontien group, is interesting for its frescoes in Siamese style of the Vedic gods of India and for the fact that it has served as the residence, at one time or another, of the last four reigning monarchs of Thailand beginning with Rama VI. The first Boromabiman was built by King Mongkut, but was subsequently dismantled during the reign of King Chulalongkorn and the present structure erected on nearly the same site. Following his coronation, King Rama VI altered the structure somewhat, added the frescoes and occupied it as his residence. The palace commands a beautiful view of the Royal Chapel.

The Wat Phra Keo (Temple of the Emerald Buddha) is just a bit north of the Mahamontien buildings, through a connecting gateway. It is probably the most famous place in Thailand, and the Assembly Hall serves as the king's private chapel. Therein is the Emerald Buddha, the most sacred image to be found in all of Thailand. Temple bells hang from the eves of the temple and the gentle tones of the bells, stirred by the breeze, provide a fitting prelude to the visual delights within.

The Buddha image itself is about 24 inches high and is placed high on a golden altar. In spite of its name, it is not actually emerald but was carved from a single piece of polished green jasper (a semiprecious form of quartz) and very possibly came originally from Ceylon. The image was discovered in Chiang Mai in 1436. As in the case of the Golden Buddha, the precious image within was discovered when its outer plaster covering became cracked. From Chiang Mai it was moved to Lampang, back to Chiang Mai, then to Luang Prabang and finally to Vientiane in Laos, from whence it was brought back to Thailand during the reign of King Takh Sin. His successor, Rama I, placed it in the royal chapel when it was constructed in 1784. The king himself changes the gem-encrusted robes of the image three times a year, a change of raiment for each of the three seasons.

Murals on the walls within the building depict the life story of the Buddha. Elsewhere episodes from the *Ramakien* are represented, and the inlaid mother-of-pearl door panels of the chapel exhibit work of the finest craftsmanship.

On the upper terrace of the chapel grounds there are several other noteworthy structures, among them the giant golden chedi, the Pantheon containing statues of past rulers of the present dynasty and a fascinating model of Ankor Wat that was presented as a gift to King Mongkut. Here and there, scattered about among these monuments, there are models of elephants and mythological creatures.

English-speaking Westerners commonly refer to the *wat* as a *temple*. This is not strictly correct. A wat is a monastery, or chapel, if as in the case of the Wat Phra Keo no monks live there, and connotes the entire complex of buildings. Thus a wat typically contains the *bot* where the monks worship and meditate and which houses the main Buddha image; a *viharn*, where sacred objects may be kept and the people come to worship; a shrine, the bell-shaped *chedi* wherein there may be a sacred Buddha relic; and the *prang*, a tower shaped like a corncob. Another building will provide living quarters for the monks, and still another may house the village school.

There are 250 to 300 wats or temples in Bangkok alone, and thousands in the whole of Thailand. They provide a living museum of Thai architecture and much of the country's art and culture. In the provinces they provide the focus of community life. The visitor is certain to see several during even the shortest stay.

A reclining Buddha, some 160 feet long and nearly 40 feet high, may be seen in the *Wat Po* (temple of the Reclining Buddha). The image is said to represent the dying Buddha. This Wat, the largest in Bangkok, has extensive grounds and a number of chedis and viharns. In the galleries surrounding the bot there are nearly 400 sitting Buddha images. There are scenes from the *Ramayana* in basrelief on marble panels around the bot which were brought here from the ruins of Ayutthaya. The life of Lord Buddha is depicted in murals on the walls within. Several ages and capitals in Thai history are represented by as many Buddha images. A sitting Buddha in the bot came from an ancient monastery in Thonburi; others came from Sukhothai and from Ayutthaya. Some fine temple rubbings come from the Wat Po, and students are often seen here, busy with their sketching pads.

The *Wat Trimitr* (Temple of the Golden Buddha) is small. There is an interesting story concerning the Buddha image within. It was moved from an abandoned monastery downtown to the Wat Trimitr some years ago. There wasn't a suitable hall to house it, and it was kept in a shed on the temple grounds for some years. The surface of the image appeared to be of plaster or concrete, and it was extremely heavy and difficult to move. In the course of moving it into a new temple hall, it fell from a crane and crashed to the ground. That night a heavy rain fell, and the next morning the image was seen to be cracked and splattered with mud. The abbot, surveying the damage, discovered through the cracks that the plaster was only an exterior covering—further investigation revealed that inside was an image of gold! The image is ten feet high and weights 5½ tons. Its size is accentuated by the relatively small hall in which it is placed. It was probably cast during the Sukhothai period (1238-1378 A.D.) and may have been covered with plaster to conceal its true value from invaders.

The *Wat Arun* (Temple of the Dawn) is across the river in Thonburi, and its great central spire can be seen for a great distance. The temple is guarded by massive stone temple dogs and an assortment of gargoyles and stern-faced gods. These images, it is believed, came from China. The exterior is covered with thousands of tiny pieces of colored porcelain.

It was in Thonburi that King Takh Sin established his capital after the fall of Ayutthaya. He restored an older monastery on the site of Wat Arun. Later, in the reigns of King Rama II and King Rama III, the great tower (prang) and four smaller ones were constructed. They are made of brick covered with stucco into which bits of colored porcelain have been imbedded. Siva's trident tops each tower. In the central tower there are figures of the Indian god Indra atop Erawan (a three-headed elephant), and elsewhere there are moon gods seated on white horses, angels and demons and other figures from the rich tradition of the Thais. A long steep climb brings one to the balcony of the large central tower. From this vantage point one can view the Grand Palace, the royal chapel, the Wat Po and Bangkok across the river. There is a boat landing on the river at the edge of the temple grounds, and it is possible to return to the Bangkok side by boat if one is so inclined. The crossing requires only a few minutes.

The *Wat Sutat* is one of the largest of Bangkok's monasteries. It was constructed during the reigns of the first three rulers of the present dynasty. There are two main buildings, the bot and viharn, enclosed in a courtyard formed by covered galleries housing a number of seated Buddha images. In front of the monastery, in Great Swing Square, stands a giant swing made of two towering teak pillars and an ornate crossbar and painted a brilliant red. In years gone by it was used in the Swing Festival. This festival is entirely Brahmanic in origin. In the Hindu faith it is believed that the god Siva once a year comes to visit the world for 10 days. For the god's amusement the four guardians of the earth come to prepare circus acts, and the great swing was a part of the circus props used to entertain him. The festival is no longer held here, and the swing itself has been removed, but the gigantic supports remain.

To the east of the old Bangkok city wall is the *Wat Sraket* and the Golden Mount. The latter is a man-made hill topped by a chedi which enshrines a relic of the Lord Buddha. Many pious Buddhists have made the pilgrimage to this holy shrine. It was King Mongkut who finally built the great mount, which is similar to the Golden Mount in Ayutthaya, after an earlier attempt during the rule of King Rama III failed. It is possible to climb the steps to the summit, and aside from the religious significance of the chedi there are excellent views of the City in every direction.

The *Wat Benchamaborpit* (Marble Monastery) provides an outstanding example of modern Thai architecture. This beautiful little monastery was built in 1899 by royal order in the reign of King Chulalongkorn. It sits on the bank of a small klong and is in the general vicinity of the King's Palace and the National Assembly Hall. The construction is of gleaming white Italian marble, roofed with golden Chinese tile. The gables represent various mythological figures—Vishnu astride a garuda, the traditional Thai erawan, and on another the Buddhist Wheel of Law. Two huge marble lions guard the main entrance. In the inner courtyard numerous bronze Buddha images line the cloister walls, and there is a sacred Bo tree grown from a sapling brought from Buddha Gaya in India at the beginning of the century. The royal pavilion used by King Chulalongkorn when he was a monk at the Wat Phra Keo has been moved here and is just across the picturesque little footbridge that spans the klong. The quiet interior of the bot contains a magnificent image of the Buddha. The atmosphere is especially solemn and seems literally charged with the spiritual beauty of the Buddhist faith.

The grounds of Chitlatda Palace are just to the northeast of Benchamaborpit. Here sentries will be seen posted along the moat surrounding the grounds, for this is the actual residence of King Bhumibol. In the opposite direction, along Si Ayutthaya Road, there is a parade ground with an equestrian statue of King Chulalongkorn, and behind that is National Assembly Hall.

This building was originally the Throne Hall. It is an imposing structure, now used for the sessions of the legislature, and was built of Italian marble in the years 1907-1915. Arrangements can be made by telephone for a visit to the building, and it is customary to address a letter to the Secretary formally requesting permission to tour the Hall. Among the several offices in the building are those of the Chairman and Vice Chairman and there is an ambassadors' room. In the legislative chamber itself there are chairs for each member of the Assembly, nearly 300 now. For the present, until the new constitution is put into effect, there is no Senate. High up on the ceilings there are huge murals in each of which one of the first five rulers of the reigning Chakri dynasty is the central figure. The throne of the king, upon which he is seated when attending the Assembly, may also be viewed. At the front of the building there is a small balcony from which the king greets his people on the parade ground below.

Returning to the vicinity of the Grand Palace, there is a large open field which borders on the Palace walls. This is the Pramane Grounds, at one time the site of royal cremations and now used for a variety of purposes not the least of which is the weekend market. From early on Saturday morning, through the following day, there are scores and scores of vendors tending small stalls offering all sorts of things—household wares, flowers, fish, birds, food, woodcarvings, leather goods, cloth, souvenirs, piles of native fruits, paper bags, and one may even consult a fortune teller here. The Pramane Grounds may also be the scene of kite-flying contests, and the Ploughing Ceremony is held here each year in May in order to give the farmers the signal that the auspicious date has come to start ploughing for the new rice crop.

The National Theatre, National Museum and the buildings of Thammasart University are to be seen just to the west. Of the Thai universities, Chulalongkorn is the oldest and Thammasat the largest. Other institutions of higher learning provide training in medicine, the fine arts and agriculture. Traditionally education of the young was in the hands of the Buddhist clergy. While many primary schools are still physically a part of the wats, they are now provided by the government and attendance for the first four years is compulsory. Secondary schools provide further education in two 3-year programs. After completing these ten years of schooling, the student must take a further two-year course if he wishes to go on to one of the universities.

For the visitor who seeks a sweeping view of Siamese history and culture in short compass, a visit to the National Museum can be a most rewarding experience. Its several buildings house exhibits from every period which reflect the long cultural, religious and economic development of the kingdom. Archeological finds provide some index to the prehistory of the area as well.

The oldest buildings of the museum date from the founding of the capital in 1782 when they were constructed as the palace of the Second King. It was the practice up until the time of Rama V for a Second King to be designated as Prince Successor. The title was *Prince of the Wang Na.* This prince had his own palace and retainers and received a share of the royal revenue. King Chulalongkorn discontinued the title and later set aside three of the old palace buildings for use as a museum. The present land of the Museum was a part of the original palace grounds and was later conveyed to the Museum, along with the remaining palace buildings, by King Prajadhipok in 1926. Two new buildings were added to the complex and officially dedicated in 1967.

The prehistoric specimens on display date from the Pleistocene epoch onward. There are Mesolithic and Neolithic tools discovered in Kanchanaburi province and other pieces of pottery and artifacts which provide ample evidence of the existence of prehistoric man within the area of the present-day kingdom.

While most of the exhibits are from Thailand, the Asian gallery contains art objects from most of the other Asian countries and even a few from the Roman world. There is a sufficiently large number of specimens to enable one to trace the development of major periods beginning with the early Funan and going on through the Dvaravati, Srivijaya, Khmer and Chiang Saen periods to the evolvement of the distinctly Siamese cultural forms of the Sukhothai, Ayutthaya and Bangkok periods.

The old central buildings contain a number of rooms which were originally the personal living apartments of the Wang Na. Here there are now collections of ancient weapons and regalia, costumes, theatrical masks, musical instruments, boats, and hundreds of other objects which fairly defy classification.

The "Red House," once the living quarters of the sister of King Rama I and later used by the consort of Rama II, is also to be seen with its early Bangkok furnishings and, indeed, some of the very belongings of its royal occupants.

The Royal State Palanquin used to convey the present king in procession to his coronation is exhibited, and in the Royal Chapel building there is the much-venerated Phra Buddha Sihing, a Buddha image held sacred by the Thais since the early years of Sukhothai.

For fear that the stranger to Bangkok should conclude from these few pages that the city holds only Buddhist monasteries, some palaces and a museum, let the reader be assured that there is a great variety of things to see and do. The Suan Pakkad Palace with its interesting lacquer pavilion provides a fine example of Thai architecture and houses a collection of rare antiques. There are also antiques and other objects of art in Jim Thompson's house, which is open to the public. After World War II, Thompson was instrumental in reviving the Thai silk industry. A few years ago he disappeared while on holiday in the Malaysian hill country. In spite of a search on an international scale, the mystery of his disappearance has never been solved.

A snake farm at the Pasteur Institute contains both harmless and poisonous species of snakes, including the deadly cobras. The extraction of venom, for the preparation of vaccines, may be observed.

In the Bangkok area there are a couple of Disney-like recreation areas. One offers "Thailand in Miniature," everything from the story of rice cultivation and work elephants to folk dances and Thai boxing. The other is a popular resort area with extensive flower gardens, two swimming pools, five restaurants and afternoon shows featuring not only classical dancing, sword fighting and village handicrafts, but also, as the tourist literature proclaims, "Buddhist ordination and bull fighting are performed with admission of 100 Baht per head." That is, indeed, something for everyone!

A number of the hotels and restaurants in Bangkok provide daily programs of Thai classical dancing. Innumerable nightclubs and open air restaurants offer entertainment in a contemporary vein. For the sportsman there are several golf courses, horse racing, and Thai boxing is both exciting and unusual. In this sport the boxers fight with fists, knees, elbows and feet!

Thais are a gregarious people. They are happiest when giving or attending a party. Their desire for the company of others prevails on the golf course as well. In America golf is usually played with a foursome. There is a maximum of four players. Not so in Thailand. A foursome simply doesn't give the Thai the company he needs. Accordingly it is not uncommon to find a "fourteensome" or even a "sixteensome" moving around the course in a long serpentine formation, all playing the same game at the same time, golf balls flying thick through the air. Just how one would play through such a formation is difficult to imagine.

Ayutthaya, the old capital of Thailand, is about 50 miles north of Bangkok and the site of ancient ruins as fabulous as those of Angkor Wat in neighboring Cambodia. The trip can be easily made by auto, bus, train or by boat up the river.

Enroute, the former Royal Summer Palace at Bang Pa-In is worth a visit. Here, in addition to structures in purely Thai architectural style, there are two buildings in Grecian style, a Gothic church and a replica of the Peking Palace. Broad tree-lined walks through the gardens accent the quiet beauty of the place, and there is a lovely pavilion poised over the water of a small lake like an Oriental gem in a setting of antique silver. The palace is no longer in use as a royal residence.

Ayutthaya was named after Ayodhya, the fabled city in northern India from which Rama set out to conquer Ceylon as recounted in the ancient Hindu epic, the *Ramayana*. It was the capital of Thailand from 1350 until it was destroyed by the Burmese in 1767. In its days of glory it is said to have had a population larger than that of contemporary European capitals. Founded by a Prince of U-Thong, later proclaimed king with the title of Rama Tibodi, the city was situated on an island formed by three rivers. The Lopburi River flows on the north, the Pasak River on the east, and the Menam Chao Phraya on the west and south. In its days of power, the Kingdom of Ayutthaya absorbed the earlier Sukhothai kingdom and extended over central Thailand including Lopburi, Ratburi and Petchaburi, up to the border of Chiang Mai in the north, and into the southern peninsula including Nakhon Si Thammarat and even as far as Malacca in the south of modern Malaysia. To the east the rule of Ayutthaya extended deep into what is now Cambodia, including the capital of Angkor Thom.

The Ayutthayan kings frequently had to defend the kingdom from the rulers of Chiang Mai in the north, but it was with the Burmese that the greatest troubles arose. The wars with Burma commenced in the middle of the sixteenth century and continued, off and on, for more than 200 years. Finally, early in 1766 a huge invasion army, reinforced by a Burmese northern army from Chiang Mai, arrived before the walls of the city. The siege lasted for many months. Outer defensive works were gradually taken and the streets of the capital came under the fire of Burmese cannon. Food supplies of the defenders were depleted. An epidemic raged, and early in the following year a fire destroyed thousands of dwellings. Faced literally with starvation, the defenders held out until April 1767 when, after fourteen months, the attackers finally breached the walls and entered the city. The palaces and other principal buildings were put to the torch. Although the Burmese were also Buddhists, they spared not even the monasteries. Buddha images were broken up and melted for their gold. People were beaten, tortured and killed to get them to reveal their treasures. The king fled and his ultimate fate remains unknown. Tens of thousands of others, among them the royal family, members of the court and officials, were carried off to Burma along with vast amounts of treasure and booty.

The city was a ruins. Now, spread out over an area of some 40 square miles, the crumbling walls of once glorious palaces and temples, the remains of some chedis, and here and there some stone Buddha images, give mute testimony to the once great power and glory of this ancient city. Few of the structures have been restored. The Chao Sam Phraya National Museum contains a number of bronze Buddha images, some woodcarved doors and altar sets, and a large collection of local artifacts. Some excavation work is underway. Elsewhere, and for the most part, vegetation threatens to slowly engulf what little remains of these earlier works of man.

The royal palace consisted of five large buildings, the Viharn Somdet, Sunpet Prasad, Suriyart Amarin, Chakravat Paichayon, Banyong Ratanas and Trimukh. All of these were completely destroyed, and, with the exception of the Trimukh building, which was restored by King Chulalongkorn in 1907, nothing now remains but a few brick foundations and partial walls. The royal chapel, the Phra Sri Sanpet monastery, was also destroyed. It once contained a great standing Buddha image, installed in 1500 A.D., but this too perished when it was fired by the Burmese to recover its gold covering.

One of the most impressive of the ruins is the Phra Chedi Chai-Mongkol, which was built by King Naresuan following his victory over the Burmese crown prince in 1592. The base of the great chedi is partially covered with vegetation, the walls are crumbling and the bases of huge supporting columns provide only a suggestion of the original size and beauty of the structure. There are still to be seen, however, the rows of seated Buddha images which surrounded the chedi on four sides.

The Wat Suwan Dararam is a more recent structure built by the grandfather of the first Chakri king, Rama I, and it has long been connected with the present ruling dynasty. The walls of the bot are covered with paintings which depict events in the life of the Buddha, while within the viharn there are paintings of important episodes in Thai history.

Elsewhere there are the ruins of the Wat Maha Dhat, one of the most extensive monasteries in Ayutthaya. It is believed to have been constructed in 1347 A.D. A number of excavations carried on by the government nearly twenty years ago resulted in the discovery of several ancient treasures, among them relics of the Lord Buddha, some golden images of the Buddha, votive tablets and gem-encrusted golden lanterns. The ruins of the wat, which was totally destroyed in the sack of 1767, cover a large area.

Another ruin is that of the Wat Rajaburana. It was built in the 15th century by King Boromaraja in memory of his two elder brothers. The latter, upon the death of the king, their father, engaged in mortal combat to decide which should have the throne. They slew each other simultaneously, and their younger brother thereupon became king.

The Phra Chedi Sri Suriyothai, on the banks of the Menam Chao Phraya, was erected by King Chakrapat to honor his brave queen who risked and lost her life in defense of her royal husband. This was in the mid-16th century when the Burmese besieged the capital for the first time. The Queen, wearing armor and mounted on a war elephant, fought side by side with the king's men when he was hard pressed in fierce fighting with the enemy at the city wall.

Continuing northward from Ayutthaya, the town of Lop Buri is situated about 90 miles (154 kms.) from Bangkok. It is an ancient place and is of particular interest because of its importance during the Dvaravati period. There are several wats and shrines in the area. The Wat Phra Sri Ratana Maha Dhat dates from the time of Khmer rule in the 12th century and contains chedis and prangs which are interesting architecturally, and there are also some fine Buddha images. Lop Buri served for a time as the capital and was perhaps selected because it is further up the river where the water is more shallow and the boats of the European colonial powers could not penetrate. Several buildings, including a residence and chapel, which were constructed to accommodate the first French ambassador sent to the kingdom by King Louis XIV, during the reign of King Narai, are still standing. The Phra Karn Shrine is none the less interesting for the fact that it is a reconstruction of a reconstruction. The original shrine was built by the Khmers. Later, during the Ayutthaya period, the remains of this shrine were rebuilt as a Buddhist monastery, and then in the 1950's the shrine was once again reconstructed as it presently appears. The Prang Sam Yod (Sacred Three-Spire Pagoda) was probably also the work of the Khmers. A Hindu shrine, already centuries old in the time of King Narai, may have been dedicated to the worship of Siva. The local museum, housed in the Phra Narai Rachanives Palace, contains some excellent specimens of art works and other artifacts of the Dvaravati period.

The first capital of the Thais was Sukhothai, and this lies still further to the north, some 544 kms. from Bangkok. It is not on the rail line, but is accessible by auto or bus. The ruins of palaces and temples can only hint at the grandeur that was once here. The Wat Maha Dhat served as the Royal Chapel during the Sukhothai period; and among the other wats here are the Wat Sra Sri, with its spired chedi; and the Wat Phra Badh Noi, notable for its chedi of rather unusual design and for a stone footprint of the Lord Buddha. At the Wat Chetupon, the ceiling of the viharn represents the story of a previous incarnation of the Buddha.

Still further north, well up toward the border with Burma, is Chiang Mai, the country's second-largest city. The name applies as well to the province. It is about 800 kms. north of Bangkok. It can be reached by auto, over good highways, and there are several flights daily to and from Bangkok via Thai Airways. There is also an excellent overnight express train service with airconditioned sleepers. The train leaves Bangkok in the late afternoon, and there is ample sunlight left for watching the countryside slide by during dinner and the early hours of the evening. Upon arising early the following morning, the traveler will find himself high up in the hill country south of Chiang Mai. The track winds along the hillsides and through the low mountains, and there are superb views looking down on the lush green forests below. This is teak country, and in the United States, of course, teak is a highly valued and often expensive hardwood widely used in the making of fine furniture, boat decks and for other purposes where a beautiful wood finish is desired. Locally the wood finds more prosaic uses as evidenced by the neatly stacked piles of teak railroad ties to be seen at way stations along the route.

Chiang Mai was founded by King Mengrai as his capital city, and some portions of the 13th century city wall still exist. Tradition has it that the labor of 90,000 workers was employed in building the wall and that it was completed in only four months. The temperatures are somewhat cooler than in Bangkok, and there is infinitely less traffic and bustle than in the capital. The atmosphere is almost rural and the pace of living quite leisurely.

There are mountains and teak forests near by, rushing mountain streams and waterfalls. One need but contemplate a Chiang Mai maiden to find true beauty of another kind. The women of these parts are especially noted for their beauty. Master craftsmen in the area produce fine handwoven fabrics, silver jewelry, colorful painted umbrellas and intricate woodcarvings.

There are several noteworthy temples in the immediate area. The Wat Phra Singh dates from the mid-14th century and houses a venerated Buddha image. Wat Phra Tadt Doy Suthep was built high on a mountain top from which there are excellent views of the countryside. This Wat possesses several relics of the Buddha. Another, the Wat Suan Dork, also contains relics of the Buddha and the remains of members of the old Chiang Mai royal families. The Wat Kao Tue contains one of the largest Buddha images ever cast in bronze, and the Wat Chiang Mai, built around 1300, is the oldest of all and the one-time residence of the founder of Chiang Mai, King Mengrai.

Bhubing Palace, the summer palace of the royal family, is just a bit beyond Doy Sutep.

A tour of the teak forests affords an opportunity of watching work elephants moving the huge teak logs. The very nature of the logging operation and the rough forest country virtually preclude the use of mechanized equipment, and so the elephants continue to bring out the logs as they have for centuries past. A visit to Mae Klang Falls or the Mae Sa Cascades provides another and different view of the natural beauty of the area.

While all Thais enjoy festival times of year, the people of Chiang Mai seem to observe these periods with a special zest. In April they celebrate Song-kran, the Thai New Year, with the so-called water festival. Originally it was the custom, at this time of year, to pour water with very considerable formality upon the hands of elders while seeking their blessing. Nowadays the practice seems to be to drench everyone in sight. Late in the year, in November, there is the Festival of Lights, Loy Krathong. Hundreds and hundreds of candles, each in a tiny boat, are floated down the Mae Ping River which runs through the city. This custom is pursued as one manner of paying homage to the Buddha, and it also reflects the more primitive practice of giving thanks to the Water Goddess.

There are a number of hilltribe settlements in the vicinity of Chiang Mai, and a visit to any of them reveals a culture quite different from that of the Thais. The tribes differ in language and customs as well. In particular, there are six tribes distributed over several provinces in northern Thailand. They are the Meo, Akha, Lisus, Lahu, Yao and Karen. In times past many of these people earned their livelihood by the cultivation of opium, but in recent years the government has encouraged them to adopt other agricultural pursuits and they now raise rice, maize, chili, cotton and tobacco. Domestic animals are also raised. The Lahu tribe is less inclined toward agriculture and prefers hunting; they move around frequently and raise crops only when it is necessary for their existence. The Akha people build their houses and villages high up in the mountains, and the Yaos, who came originally from Central China, have been slow to lose their ancient customs and still observe the Chinese New Year. A number of the tribes believe in spirits, and in at least one tribe there are witch doctors.

The Karen settlements aren't the closest to Chiang Mai, of the tribal villages, but a drive out to see these people enables the traveler to see several other interesting areas as well. There are about 70,000 Karens living in the valleys of Chiang Mai, Mae Hongson, Chiang Rai and Lampoon provinces.

One route to a White Karen village (there are "red" and "black" Karen people as well, so-called because of their skin shading), passes along the old Chiang Mai to Bangkok road, which is lined for long stretches with gum trees. The way passes the Wat Phra Dhat Hari-Poonchai, in Lampoon province. This is one of the most sacred monuments in the north, and it was built in the year 1157. A great brass gong on the monastery grounds is said to have been cast in the reign of the first king of Chiang Mai. It measures some five or six feet in diameter.

There are many malyai (longan) orchards in this area, and, in addition to the usual rice culture, garlic is raised in great quantities. Now and again domed ovens will be observed along the way. These are used to produce charcoal, which is sold in baskets along the road side, a basket for as little as three or four Bahts.

Further along is the village of Pasang, which has the local reputation, at least, of being "the town of beautiful girls." In the village center, a long row of pedicabs — the lineal descendants of the rick-shaw — will be observed, along with a group of lounging local swains, perhaps pondering the question of which pedicab to take after which girl. This is also a center for the weaving of cottons and silks on the hand looms, of which there are a great many in the area. It is a painstaking job, especially when the colored threads have to be worked into the cloth to produce sometimes quite intricate designs.

The Wat Jamadevi is not far away and here there is a particularly interesting chedi in Burmese architectural style, quite different from those usually seen in other parts of the country.

The Karen tribal settlement is typically deep in the forest and scarcely accessible by auto. They are a shy people, but it usually isn't very long until a group of adventurous small boys will come up to examine the visitor and, with two fingers to the lips and considerable huffing and puffing, convey the idea that they would like to have a cigarette. The people raise tobacco and are fond of rolling their own or smoking a pipe. A charming little girl, no more than 8 or 9 years old, comes up the village path solemnly puffing on an old pipe. Moments later a wrinkled old woman will move slowly down the path, also smoking a pipe. Underneath one of the huts, out of the sun and hard at work over the loom, there is a most attractive girl in her late teens — smoking a pipe! The people live in leaf-roofed huts, elevated several feet above the ground, and pigs, chickens and dogs have the run of the village. Tribal costumes are colorful, but the very youngest of the tribe dispense with tribal costumes, and costumes of any sort, to romp about the village quite naked.

The tribes are the object of intensive study at the Tribal Research Center at the University of Chiang Mai. The information being collected there has not only added to knowledge of ethnological groups and migratory patterns, but it has also enabled the government to formulate policies and programs for the benefit of the tribes.

For the return trip to the Bangkok area, there are several flights operated by the domestic airline. Local hotels provide bus service to the airport. Departure of the bus from the hotel may be somewhat later than scheduled, and arrival at the airport may be at just about the time the flight is scheduled to depart. However, any sort of nervous inquiry as to whether the bus will arrive early enough will be met with the explanation that while the bus does indeed depart late and may arrive somewhat late at the airport, it is equally true that the flight may depart late, so that everything works out very well in the end. So it does. *Mai pen rai!*

On a map, Thailand looks something like the head and trunk of an elephant. Chiang Mai is well up in the north at the top of the head,

Bangkok is centrally located, and the long trunk extends southward into the Malay peninsula. Just as there are some differences in custom and even in the pronunciation of the language in the north, as compared with the Bangkok area, so there are other differences in the south. All of the Thais share the same basic culture and language, but these regional differences lend a distinctive character to these particular areas. Spoken Thai in the deep south, in Nakhon Si Thammarat or in Songkhla for example, is slightly different from the "middle Thai" spoken in Bangkok.

The physical characteristics of the south country are also very different. The mountainous area in the north gives away to the flat, rice-growing, central plains surrounding the capital. As one travels southward, into the peninsula, there are again mountain ranges. There are still many rice fields, but to these are added vast coconut groves, especially north of the Nakhon Si Thammarat area, extensive rubber plantations further to the south, and on the western side of the peninsula toward the Malaysian border there are many tin mines.

South of Bangkok along the Gulf of Thailand, there are some beautiful resort areas. Pattaya is one of the most popular beaches, and it is only about 90 miles southeast of the capital. Upper-income Thais trek down here regularly, and there are likely to be other visitors and vacationers from almost anywhere. Accommodations range from airconditioned hotel rooms to charming little teak houses, but the main things, of course, are the sand and the sun. Boats are available for trips to the offshore islands, and one can fish, snorkel, water ski, sail, golf, or go horseback riding. All of these activities have palm-studded beaches and the sandy shoreline as a backdrop. Bangsaen is another popular resort, with a fisherman's village and some small oyster farms in the area. For the golfer, there is a good 18-hole course only a few minutes away at Bang Phra.

Over on the west side of the Gulf there is Hua Hin, which has some beautiful tropical beaches. It is the summer residence of the royal family. The Songkhla area, in the extreme south, also has a number of resorts. There are, or course, many more scattered about in the south, on both sides of the peninsula.

Thai Airways maintains service to most of the cities in the southern area, or the visitor may prefer to drive or take a train. There is also steamship service from Bangkok to Songkhla.

The main highway passes down the eastern peninsular coast to Phet Buri and Hua Hin, already mentioned, and then to Prachuab

Khirikhan. The mountainous area on the Burmese border is frequently visible from the highway, and at Prachuab there are more beaches, some interesting off-shore islands and strangely shaped mountains. Further south, in the vicinity of Chum Phon, one can continue on the highway along the east coast side to Surat Thani and on to Nakhon Si Thammarat, or cross the peninsula to the western side. The latter route lies along the Kra River, which forms the border here between Thailand and Burma, and then continuing further south there is the Indian Ocean. Although it lies some kilometers to the south of the main highway, the island of Phuket offers some seldom-visited beaches and is a center of tin mining and rubber plantations. The highway then across the peninsula to the eastern side, to Phattalung, Haadyai and Songkhla. The Malaysian border is only a few miles beyond.

The entire southern coastal area is virtually unspoiled. There are fishing villages, miles of quiet beaches, nearby mountains, and many small offshore islands, wooded coves and coral reefs.

For the traveler who prefers the train, there is an international express service, which leaves Bangkok three times a week, crosses the entire peninsula form north to south and connects with the service of Malayan Railways to Penang (Butterworth), Kuala Lumpur and Singapore. The train leaves Bangkok in late afternoon, pulls out of the station headed north, skirting the edge of the Chitlatda Palace grounds, until, just past the Bangsue station, it turns sharply west and then crosses the Chao Phraya River.

Now and again one can observe the little "spirit houses" which are perched on poles or pedestals in the yards of homes which can be seen from the train car. These miniature houses are built by Thai householders as an abode for the *Chao Ti*, the spirit who rules the plot of ground upon which the dwelling has been constructed. Periodic offerings of food, flowers and incense are placed by the spirit house for the spirit in order to retain his goodwill. Not only do individual dwellings have such spirit houses but also the great modern hotels and other buildings. Out in the country, as Bangkok fades into the distance, the spirit houses on the farmers' holdings may be quite rustic. The changing scene now offers luxuriant vegetation, frequently heavy growth of palms, flat rice fields and innumerable farms.

After crossing the Menam Tha Chin, the train pulls into Nakhon Pathom. This is the oldest city in the country, and it was a capital centuries ago during the period of the Dvaravati Empire. Buddhism was first introduced into Thailand at this place. The influence of the Gupta period of India (317-607) is to be noted in several examples of architecture and Buddha images. The most noteworthy monument in Nakhon Pathom is the great golden chedi, the Phra Pathom Chedi, which rises almost 380 feet from the ground. Late in the afternoon, bathed in the golden rays of the setting sun, it is a most impressive sight. Its spire can be seen for miles around. The chedi, which resembles an enormous inverted bowl surfaced with golden tile, is a reconstruction which was initiated by King Mongkut in the mid-19th century and finally completed during the reign of King Chulalongkorn in 1870. It is the largest, highest and oldest chedi in the land.

Some kilometers northwest of Nakorn Pathom is the bridge on the River Kwai, familiar to many from the motion picture by that name. It is in Kanchanaburi province, which is an area of heavy jungle and rough hill country. The bridge was built during World War II at the cost of many lives of British and other prisoners of war sent here by the Japanese. The cementery at Kanchanaburi contains the graves of British, Indian, Australian and Dutch soldiers who died while building the so-called "Death Railway" during the war.

After crossing the Mae Klong, the track heads due south to Raj Buri and into Phet Buri (Petchburi). The ending of the names of many Thai towns is "Buri"—Raj Buri, Phet Buri, Kanchanaburi, Chantaburi, Lop Buri, Singha Buri, and so on. The word means "town," and it is curious that half-way around the world we also have in England and America such towns and cities as Canterbury, Waterbury, and the like. The endings are the same, and a scholar in the linguistics field could possibly trace the common origin of the word. Around Pet Buri there are numerous caves in the limestone hills, and some of these have become Buddhist shrines. The palace of King Mongkut (Rama IV) is also here.

The train route follows the east coast, along the Gulf of Thailand through Prachuab Khirikhan, Chum Phon to the vicinity of Surat Thani, where for the traveler on the international express the dawn of the new day begins to break. The countryside now has an increasing number of palm trees and there are long stretches of jungle vegetation as well as the familiar rice fields. There are a number of small way stations; Ban Na, Na Sarn, and Cha Wan. People are up and about. The farmers are already working in the rice paddies. Long straight rows of rubber trees run almost up to the railway tracks.

There are stretches of dark green, lush rain forest. Off to the east there is a range of low mountains with clouds sitting atop particularly high peaks, and a bit further on a couple of sugarloaf mountain formations jutting up quite unexpectedly from the otherwise flat rice fields, as if deposited there quite unintentionally or perhaps simply left over from the forming of a nearby range.

Tung Song Junction is next, and ordinarily the traveler on the express continues on through Phattalung and Haadyai to the Malaysian border.

Alternatively, one can leave the train at Tung Song and by change of train, or taxi, make a visit to Nakhon Si Thammarat, which is the capital of the province of that name. Because taxi fares are so inexpensive, by Western standards, it is tempting to make the trip by cab. This has the added advantage of enabling one to stop along the way to admire a view, watch the water buffalo and oxen at work in the fields or make a visit to one of the villages.

Nakhon Si Thammarat is off the beaten path and still not much frequented by tourists. Seemingly, it has been less influenced by Western ways than some other parts of the country. The Wat Mahathat, one of the oldest monasteries in Thailand, is located here. Sacred relics of the Lord Buddha are preserved in the chedi, the towering spire of which is reputed to cast no shadow! The town itself is not large and here one can observe provincial life at first hand.

As already mentioned, the majority of the people of the country live in small villages. It is perhaps more in this environment, rather than along the modern avenues of the capital city, that one can appreciate the true nature of the Thai. The author of this book was greeted in a small village, not so many kilometers from Nakhon Si Thammmart, by a Thai whom he had known for several years in New York while the latter was pursuing graduate studies there.

The village is very small, a score of houses, a school, the wat. Not far from the coast, it is situated in one of the most beautiful areas to be found anywhere in the land. There is some heavy rain forest in the area and to the west a string of low mountains, forest-covered, with early-morning vapor drifting down the valleys, and the sun now and again obscured by bluish-black clouds with a silvery-gold edging. The village sits astride the hard-surfaced road that comes from Tung Song in the west, and continues on to Pak Panang on the coast.

The driver lets you off by the side of the road. You cross over a small klong by a rough wooden footbridge, walk a few hundred yards down a dirt path, past a couple of small rice fields, and then turn off along a further path which is lined with palm trees, banana trees and the most luxuriant tropical foliage that can be imaged. The way leads into the compound of a dwelling. It is the house of a typical Thai farmer. Built some feet above the ground, there is a large veranda with a thatch roof from which the rainwater drains into a line of huge earthenware water jars, each of which is large enough to hold one of Ali Babi's thieves. Several small containers are suspended from the edge of the roof, each containing an orchid plant. There is a separate cooking house, at the back of which sheaves of rice are neatly stacked. At the far end of the compound there is the klong, shallow now and a bit brackish, not so deep and clear as in former days. It is still deep enough for a motorboat, with its long propellor shaft, to pass in mid-morning, and a little later two Thai girls cast their fish nets into the water and soon have two sizeable fish.

Thais are the most hospitable of people, and the visit is marked by the assemblage of relatives and friends, aunts and uncles, classmates, neighbors, the village headman, the village doctor and the cantonal leader. English is not spoken nor understood, but the people like to hear the language and ask again and again for it to be spoken. There are now sixty or seventy people in the compound, their number from time to time augmented by a not inconsiderable delegation of village children, the smallest of whom have probably never before seen a white foreigner at such close quarters.

By mid-morning, three saffron-robed monks arrive from the Wat Sukum. Mats are spread for them on the veranda. One is the abbot of the monastery, an old man, yet his face reflects a youthfulness and peacefulness that is difficult to describe. Of the other two, one is also elderly and of ascetic bearing and the other a young man, tall and powerfully built. The people gather around the veranda, seated or standing, and the monks chant the precepts of the Buddha in unison. The elders of the assemblage are also seated on the veranda facing the monks. They perform the wai and now and again chant responsively in the course of the service.

Food is then brought for the monks and they eat. They will take no more solid food until the following day since it is already nearly midday. Soon thereafter they take their departure.

A very long table is then formed, with the visitor at one end and the host and the village headman at the other. A country feast is soon on the table. Authentic Thai food may not appeal to all

Western palates. It is highly seasoned with peppers and spices, but there are many dishes and courses, plenty to please the taste whatever it may be. An ample portion of rice is an essential part of the meal. There is shrimp soup, grilled shrimp, freshwater catfish which have been grilled over a charcoal fire, several other varieties of fish, chicken, young shoots, chillie sauce, green leaf vegetables and a fish sauce (*nam-pla*) used liberally for seasoning. The curry dishes have been prepared with coconut milk, and there are bananas, of which there are several varieties.

Soon after the meal a visit to the Wat Sukum is arranged. A little party sets out down the path, serpentine fashion, and moves through the village to the monastery. The bot is empty. There is a large standing image of the Buddha, a dozen feet tall, next to the outside front wall, between the two entry doors. Inside, the large seated Buddha image is the central figure on the altar, and there are several other smaller images. All is quiet. One peers into the face of the Buddha image, with its half-closed eyes, gentle smile — serene, compassionate, contemplative. Lost in contemplation, the visitor at first scarcely notices that the sun has become clouded. A strong breeze begins to slap the wood shutters against the window frames, and then there is a sudden torrential downpour. It is the rainy season. Such showers at this time of year are not usually of very long duration, and in a few minutes the strong rays of the sun are already drying off the dripping vegetation outside.

Next to the bot is the viharn, a large plain building, and to the rear other buildings which provide quarters for the monks. The abbot sends word that he wishes to receive the visitor and the party moves from the bot to the abbot's quarters, which are on a second floor of still another structure. It is a more recently constructed building with cement foundation and a large hall, on the first floor, which is empty and unfurnished. The abbot's quarters are on the second storey. Each member of the group removes his shoes and ascends the stairs. The abbot is seated on a low dais, which appears to serve also as his bed. Here there is a mat over the flooring and a small roll of a pillow. A huge Thai attendant serves steaming cups of Chinese tea.

In a few moments the abbot rises and goes into an adjoining chamber, which has the appearance of a private chapel. Again there is the Buddha image, and at the two front corners of the altar life size images of two monks, one the founder of the monastery many, many years ago. There are two young monks reclining on mats in the chapel reading from the teachings of the Lord Buddha. The abbot now returns, holding two small Buddha images of clay on a cloth in his hands. Again seated, he motions for the visitor to approach. Kneeling in front of the abbot, the visitor places his hands in a wai and bows low, demeanor appropriate for the occasion, and then receives the two small images which have been specially blessed. Thanks are conveyed in English, and while the language might not have been understand the intent certainly was.

Returning then down the stairway, shoes are reclaimed and the little group — the visitor, his Thai friend, uncles and village elders — makes its way to the school, which is also a part of the wat. A hundred or so elementary school children are romping in the play area. In a few minutes everyone is made comfortable in the school reception room, greetings are exchanged, and cigarettes and cold soda are served. The very gracious schoolmaster explains the school program and comments that he now has nearly 150 elementary school children enrolled. Except for the language of the instructional materials, the school office might have been located in one of the American states — all of the accoutrements of early learning were there, pencils, writing pads, elementary reading books and so on.

By now the day was well spent and it was time to start for Tung Song Junction and rejoin the international express for points south and Malaysia. Most of the group which had assembled earlier in the day to greet the visitor had reassembled to see him on his way. By the time the car arrived, to begin the journey to the Junction, school was out and most of the schoolmaster's charges came down to the road to take one more look at this Westerner. The road was entirely blocked, but this posed no traffic hazard since "heavy" traffic in these parts is an auto passing every half-hour or so. Looking back, as the car moved away, the visitor saw the tiny hands of the little school children, the rough hands of farmer folk who work long hours in the rice fields, and the wrinkled hands of a few village elders, all raised in farewell. The gesture was perhaps not typically Thai in form, but the feeling was . . . and it surely prompted the thought that all men are made by the same Creator and are meant to live in friendship and peace, one with another.

Chapter 4

MALAYSIA —
YESTERDAY AND TODAY

The Federation of Malaysia is Thailand's neighbor to the south. It is an independent federation of states and a member of the Commonwealth of Nations. It consists of two parts separated by 400 miles across the South China Sea. West Malaysia occupies most of the Malay peninsula, which extends for 700 miles from southern Thailand to Singapore. Its western shore is washed by the Andaman Sea (a part of the Indian Ocean) and the Strait of Malacca. On the east is the South China Sea. East Malaysia comprises Sarawak and Sabah on the north coast of Borneo.

Most of West Malaysia is covered with tropical forests, and there are mountainous areas with elevations as high as 7186 feet. Miles and miles of mangrove swamps line the coastal areas. Elsewhere there are vast stretches of white sand beaches and wave-swept crags.

The climate is equatorial and even the higher altitudes in the mountains and hilly areas offer only a few degrees of relief from year-around temperatures which range close to a mean of 81 degrees (F.). Rainfall varies from 90 to 100 inches a year.

In the tropical rain forest, which covers three-fourths of the country, there are scores of different kinds of trees, hundreds of different orchids and ferns, bamboos in the lowlands, majestic palms and mangroves.

Animal life is abundant and varied. There are still some elephants, tigers and leopards. Gaur (wild cattle) are found deep in the forests and there are even a few Sumatran rhinoceros in some of the hilly areas. There are deer, wild pigs and several species of monkeys. Add crocodiles, snakes and other reptiles including the flying lizard and the fascinating little *gekos* – and the list is but commenced. Bird life is equally abundant and diverse.

The population of Malaysia is estimated to be between nine and ten millions – more than eight million in West Malaysia. Half of the population on the peninsula are Malays, some 35% Chinese, with the rest Indians, Pakistani, Eurasians, Europeans, some aborigines and others. Many Malays are to be found in the eastern states in the villages. The Chinese tend to congregate in the cities where they keep shops or are otherwise engaged in business, and many Indian workers have gravitated to the plantations. Malaysia is thus milti-racial with the Malays and Chinese forming the two largest communities. There is a further dichotomy in that there are the urban centers in the west (with many Chinese) and the villages and agricultural areas in the east peopled mostly by Malays.

The several parts of Malaysia do not share a common history, political or cultural. Witness the subservience of the northern states to Siam, the early colonization of Penang by the British, the "separateness" of Sabah and Sarawak, the long period of Portuguese rule in Malacca. Again, the rich cultural heritage of the Indian peoples who came to Malaya was quite foreign, for example, to the Chinese merchant in Singapore.

In this book the word *Malaya* is used primarily in a geographical sense to mean the Malayan peninsula and the islands of Penang and Singapore. *Malayasia* is generally used here in a political sense as denoting the area of the present federation of states which was formed in 1963 and consists of the Straits Settlements (Penang with adjacent Province Wellesey and Malacca, but not including Singapore), the Federated Malay States (Perak, Selangor, Negri Semblian and Pahang), the former unfederated Malay states (Johore, Kedah, Perlis, Kelantan and Trengganu), and Sabah and Sarawak in Northern Borneo. Historically Singapore may well be regarded as a part of Malaysia, but since its withdrawal from that state in 1965 it is a separate sovereign country.

Ignoring the Central Asian land route between Europe and the Far East, the area has been a crossroad of east-west trade for centuries. The major sea route originated in the Red Sea or Persian Gulf, went along the west coast of India and on to Malaya. The earliest route involved debarkation at the Kra Isthmus (which is only a few miles wide at its narrowest point in the far north of the peninsula) and again boarding ship in the Gulf of Siam to continue the journey eastward. Centuries later trading ships began to sail the entire route from India, through the Malacca Strait on to China or the Indonesian islands. Malaya came to be a sort of halfway station for purposes of trade. Ships from the East brought their cargoes to the Malay entrepôts and there traded for return cargoes of goods which had been brought from the West. These same entrepôts served as collection points for local produce.

The strategic location of Malaysia in east-west trade was an important factor in the historical development of the area. Control of the Malacca Straits bestowed control of much of the trade between China and India. A ready market existed in the West for the products of the East: pepper, spices, tin, silk, tea, Chinese earthenware and porcelain, etc.

First came the Portuguese, then the Dutch, then the English. But these were not the first. The Mediterranean countries were trading with Indian ports in the early years of the Christian era, and by the third century A.D. this trade had been extended to mainland Southeast Asia. When the British came to Penang to trade for Chinese tea, silk and porcelain they were following a pattern of trade that had existed between the Far East and the Middle East since the 7th century A.D.

For centuries the rivers provided the only means of access to the interior. This fact had both economic and political implications. A Malay chief could establish a strong point at the river's mouth and easily control traffic, and hence trade, up and down the waterway. Later, miners followed these same rivers in search of tin. When rails and roads were finally constructed from the mines to the coast, the rubber planters early in the present century utilized these lines of communication in locating their plantations.

The first roads were built to provide access to the tin fields and later to the rubber plantations. There are now innumerable bus routes, and highway traffic density is third highest in Asia. The main railway lines cross the west coast states. Since the construction of a causeway across the Johore Strait, in 1923, it has been possible to travel by rail from Singapore, across Malaysia, to the Thai border, a distance of 488 miles. There is a good air-conditioned, diesel-powered train service from Kuala Lumpur to Bangkok. The Malaysian Airline System provides domestic and overseas air service.

There is an east-coast area and a west-coast area divided by a central mountain range that stretches from north to south as a natural watershed. Much of the tin mining and cultivation of rubber is in the west, between the coast and the central mountain range. In the north the economy depends heavily on rice cultivation. Elsewhere coconuts and palm oil are produced. Hardwood timber is taken from the forests. Here again, even in agriculture, there is a variety of segmented economic systems, geographically separate and to some extent even pursued by different racial groups. Thus, historically, the Chinese furnished the labor for the tin mines, Indian labor is widely employed on the rubber plantations, the Malays cultivate rice, and so on.

Most of the Malay population dwells in small villages. A small village stretches along a stream that winds down the valley. On either side there are rice fields, and then clusters of wood houses built on stilts with palm leaf thatching. Many have little gardens or an orchard. A little distance away, and higher up on the slopes, are rubber small holdings.

It is from the upper class of Malay society that most of the political leadership and civil service is recruited. As education has become more readily available, however, it is increasingly possible for those of peasant origin to become civil servants, and this trend is likely to continue in the future. If the Chinese have focused on attaining economic power, the Malays may be said to dominate the political scene.

The earliest Chinese immigration was to Singapore, Malacca and Penang. Their descendants are still referred to as the "Straits Chinese." Later waves of immigrants from China were largely dispersed throughout the Malay states. Aside from differences in origin, there is a decided cleavage in the Chinese community between those who have been English-educated and those educated in the Chinese educational system. Be that as it may, the Chinese dominate local trade and have major interests in tin, rubber and banking.

The Indian community in Malaysia traces its beginnings to migrants who came mostly from the south of India as laborers in the expanding rubber industry. Today there are many Indians in the railway service, and others are in the professions, shopkeepers and clerks.

The production of rubber is of central importance to the nation's economy. It brings in a third of the country's revenue and some 60 per cent of export earnings. The rubber tree was introduced to Malaysia from Brazil via England. More than a third of the world's supply of natural rubber comes from West Malaysia. Both large and small plantations contribute to this yield and provide livelihoods for nearly a third of a million workers.

Rubber seeds from Brazil were first planted in Malaya in 1877. After 1900 there was a great flow of British and other overseas capital into tin mining and the rubber plantations. Early in the century rubber replaced tin as the largest Malayan industry.

A typical rubber plantation may consist of several thousand acres. The young, high-yield, rubber trees with their dense foliage, are planted in long straight lines. Well before day-break the tappers are already on their way to the four or five acres they will work until midday. The latex flows most freely around dawn. Both men and women do this work. Between the rows of trees other workers wield hoes to cut down unwanted growth. Here the heat and rainfall produce a veritable jungle of vegetation if new growth is not carefully and continuously controlled.

The tapper takes a thin shaving of bark from the tree by making a diagonal cut, at an angle, a third or half around the tree trunk three or four feet from the ground. The latex flows into a cup which is fixed to the tree for the purpose. Some planters use a V-shaped cut rather than a diagonal one. These tapping cuts are repeated at various intervals depending upon the species being cultivated.

Tapping of the *Hevea brasiliensis* begins when the tree is five or six years old, and with care the latex yield will continue for ten to fifteen years, sometimes longer. Yields of up to 1,000 pounds of dry sheet rubber per acre can be realized, but such yields are very high and not common.

The latex collected in the cups is poured into pails and taken to a collecting station from whence it goes to a factory. Here it is cleaned and then coagulated into slabs. Further steps convert the material into "smoked sheet" or "pale crepe." The rubber is then baled for shipment.

The mining of tin occupies second place only to rubber in the economy. Some iron and bauxite are also mined, much of which goes to Japan.

Agricultural products of importance include rice, palm oil, coconut oil, copra and timber. The production of cocoa has been encouraged. Various other food crops are grown, among them sugar cane, tapioca, sweet potatoes and pineapples. Some livestock is raised but the output is not large. Large quantities of fish are taken from coastal waters.

From Jungle Land to Modern Nation

In a prehistoric period, peoples from the Yünnan plateau on the mainland in South China migrated southward across the Malay peninsula to Indonesia and Australasia. The first primitive Malay people were descended from Mongoloid tribes, and there are even today as many as 40,000 aborigines — remote descendants of these early peoples — living under the most primitive conditions deep in the Malayan jungles.

The first waves of migration probably reached Malaya about 2,000 years before the birth of Christ. By the beginning of the Christian era, the Malays were much under the influence of nearby India.

The Indianization of Malaya in pre-European centuries is particularly notable in the entrepôt towns where ships from both sides of the Strait met and exchanged goods. Just how, and by what routes, Indian culture penetrated Southeast Asia is not entirely clear, but penetrate it did. It was from India that the Malays received an alphabet, law, literature, the Hindu and Buddhist faiths, and such crafts as the weaving of silk and working in gold and silver.

A Hindu kingdom, Fou-nan, spread over much of the continental portion of Southeast Asia in the early Christian centuries, and there was as well a Buddhist kingdom in northern Malaya. When the Fou-nan kingdom declined it was succeeded in the north of Malaya by the kingdom of Srivijaya, which was Mahayana Buddhist.

The kingdom of Srivijaya existed from the 7th to the 14th centuries. Probably originally founded in Sumatra it spread until most of Malaya was included in the kingdom. By the 8th century these Srivijaya kings in Sumatra had taken over the smaller Malay kingdoms. Various inscriptions, some in Sanskrit and some in Malay, attest to the existence of Srivijaya as does its mention by Chinese writers. It does not appear that during its long history it was so much a land area governed by these Sumatran rulers, but rather that it was in essence a collection of Indianized entrepôt centers in the Malacca Strait area and certain of the eastern islands. Srivijaya had its roots and strength in trade. When the Chola rulers conquered the Srivijaya states it may well have been that they simply took over trade and the trading centers in these areas. It was commerce that was prized rather than land.

It was the ever-present rivalry for trade routes that brought about the downfall of Srivijaya. The Indian Chola kings several times attacked Kedah, from which the Strait of Malacca was largely controlled, and a continuing warfare was carried on with the Javanese. By the 11th century these kings, from southern India, had reduced Srivijaya to the status of a dependency.

With the Yuan dynasty in China (late 13th century) came a considerable expansion in Chinese trade. The Yuans even attempted, unsuccessfully, to take Java. In opposing this Chinese expansionism, the Majaphit empire in Java invaded Sumatra and several areas in Malaya and extended its commercial influence over the entrepôts of Srivijaya, only to be supplanted in the 15th century by the Islamic sultans of Malacca. It was this preeminence of the Malacca sultanate that was successfuly challenged by the Portuguese when they took Malacca in 1511 and ushered in a period characterized by European penetration into the region.

The kingdom of Malacca was the greatest power in Southeast Asia in the 15th century. It was founded by the ruler of Tumasek (later Singapore) in 1403. Malacca possessed a good harbor, a strong fleet and became an important center in overseas trade. In spite of attacks by the Siamese, the kingdom eventually encompassed all of Malaya, including Kedah, as well as some states in Sumatra.

The Malacca Sultanate reflected a period of Malay greatness from about 1400 A.D. until the Portuguese took over in 1511. The *Sejarah Melayu* (Malay Annals), recorded soon after the Portuguese arrived, contains a history of this great kingdom. It was from Malacca that later sultanates inherited their political form and system of aristocracy. It was during the century of Malaccan power that the Malays embraced Islam.

The founder of the royal house probably came from Tumasek, which was then a part of the Sumatran empire and from which he and his followers were forced to flee when the island was attacked by either Javanese or Siamese forces. From Malacca he was able to levy duties on ships passing through the Straits. This first ruler, Paramesvara, was recognized by the Chinese as early as 1405. As the years passed the empire expanded until it finally embraced virtually all of the Malay peninsula. Islam replaced Hinduism as the religion of the people, and the port and town of Malacca became the most important center of trade in all of Southeast Asia.

The political power wielded by the sultan over the empire stemmed from his control of the merchant community and the revenues it provided to the state. Unfortunately for the empire, early in the 16th century relations between the sultan's government and the merchants had become strained and at about the same time the Portuguese appeared on the scene.

The first Portuguese vessel arrived in 1509. The Malays had imprisoned some seamen from the vessel and this provided ample excuse for a punitive expedition against Malacca under the command of Alfonso d'Albuquerque who arrived in 1511. After a seige of some weeks, Malacca was captured. Many of the defenders fled to the south and much later set up a new capital under Malay rule in Johore.

When the Malaccan empire collapsed, the Johore sultanate was the only major power on the peninsula left to resist the Portuguese. On several occasions the Malays aided the Dutch when the latter attacked the Portuguese in Malacca. The Portuguese needed Malacca and the Strait to safeguard the Goa to Macao trade route. The Dutch wanted this strategic area since its possession meant control of much of the Asian trade. The victorious power here could monopolize tin, pepper and other exports.

After the fall of Malacca in 1511, the kingdom disintegrated. Siam assumed suzerainty over the states of Kedah, Kelantan and Trengganu. Members of the old royal line still ruled in Perak and Johore, which latter sultanate dominated the south Malay states. But the rule of Johore was eroded in the 17th and 18th centuries by invaders from Makasar and Sumatra, who gained Riouw Selangor and Negri Sembilan, and finally collapsed.

When the Portuguese took Malacca it was the greatest trade center in Southeast Asia. Indian exports were exchanged here for the spice and aromatics of the islands. Here Chinese junks came laden with silks, camphor, ironware and other goods. When the Portuguese arrived, the Malaccan empire reached from Kedah in the far north on the Thai border and Trengganu in the northeast across the Strait to several kingdoms on the island of Sumatra. Capturing Malacca and maintaining a firm control over the empire were two quite different matters as the Portuguese discovered. The displaced sultan's followers not infrequently attacked the Portuguese garrisons and shipping. Raiders from the sultanate of Acheh made numerous forays. The pretentions of the Dutch had to be contended with as well. It was this preoccupation with matters in Malacca that effectively prevented the Portuguese from playing any major role in the eastern archipelago, which was to come under Dutch influence, or in the islands further to the east where the Spanish had established themselves on Luzon.

Portuguese power and influence were not lacking, however. Throughout the 16th century they parried the Malayan offensives and for the most part maintained an uneasy peace with the Malays. They traded, or fought as occasion required, with Siam, China, Japan and the Moluccas. They were admitted to Japan in 1543, and their trade with China was legalized in 1554.

In 1564 forces from the sultanate of Acheh in northern Sumatra flooded over Johore and the weakened Malays found themselves more or less in alliance with the Achinese against Portuguese Malacca. Prior to this the Malays had sought an alliance with the Portuguese to counter the Achinese attacks, but the Portuguese were willing to see Johore overrun since it represented a potential threat to the dominance of Malacca as the leading entrepôt in the region. For more than 50 years the Achinese mounted periodic attacks on Malacca and attained a position of considerable power in the Straits. Acheh suzerainty extended to Perak, Kedah and Pahang by 1620, and they exercised effective control of Johore as well. The revival of Johore as a political power finally ended Achinese rule in 1641.

For a century the Portuguese maintained their power in Malacca. By the time the Dutch arrived early in the 17th century, Portuguese power was in decline. Their fortress at Malacca was more than once under siege. Their continual wars with Johore and Acheh had been costly, and their fanatical opposition to the Islamic faith added to the unpopularity of their regime, as did the taxes they imposed on domestic trade. They were no match for the Dutch. In 1641, Malacca was taken and the Portuguese left the peninsula.

As the Dutch penetrated the Indies they had successfully challenged Portuguese trade, and with the capture of Malacca they were now established on the peninsula itself. Under the Dutch, Malacca declined in size and importance as a trade center. It remained under the Dutch until the British took it over in 1795. During their period of ascendancy on the Malay peninsula, the Dutch sought to monopolize trade in tin and pepper, and in gold from Siak.

They collected duties from ships passing Malacca and maintained impressive naval strength in the Strait. They were not able, however, to enforce their trading claims in Kedah, the island of Phuket (Junk Ceylon) or other relatively remote areas on the peninsula, nor were they able to extend their monopolies to neighboring Johore or Selangor.

To avoid the heavy exactions of the Dutch in the Malacca Straits, much east-west trade began to use the Sunda Straits, and native trade likewise evaded Dutch controls whenever possible. The Dutch sought to impose their monopolies and were for the most part successful. The pattern was simple enough. They negotiated treaties or agreements with the native rulers which gave them both the right to purchase the produce of their lands and a similar exclusive right to supply cloth and other imported goods in their territories.

The monopolies on trade and other exactions produced deep antagonism between the Dutch and the Malays. They were, at certain times, however, more or less allied by force of circumstances. Thus they were united in their opposition to the Portuguese early in the century. In the 18th century they were again mutually in opposition to the threat of the Bugis. These people, who came from the Celebes, traded throughout the archipelago. Many began to settle along both sides of the Malacca Straits, and eventually they gained control of the Johore dynasty, which by about 1720 had its seat on Riau, south of Singapore. Other Bugis settlements were united in a new kingdom, Selangor, under a Bugis sultan. Because Riau was attracting trade that would have otherwise brought revenue to the Dutch in Malacca, the latter were willing allies of the Malays who warred on the Bugis from 1756 until 1787. This latter date marks the beginning of British involvement in the area and the decline of Dutch influence.

The British were comparatively slow in developing their relations with the Malay states. As relative latecomers they had to face competition provided by both Portuguese and Dutch traders in the area. Too, exchange of goods tended to be fragmented. Disposing of a ship's entire cargo and securing local goods in exchange was a piecemeal operation and time consuming. While British "country traders" exported tin, pepper and even elephants in the century before 1770, their trade was not in bulk. Trading visits of East-indiamen to the Malay country were infrequent and then usually made only in the course of voyages to China and elsewhere.

By about 1760, for a variety of reasons, the British began to evidence greater interest in Malaya. They desired to establish a settlement near the Malacca Strait as a major center for the concentration of Southeast Asian exports for shipment to Canton. The same center would serve as a market for British goods and might also serve as a naval base.

Several efforts to locate the proposed British entrepôt were launched. When Kuala Selangor and Riau fell to the Dutch it appeared that the latter might now dominate the Malay states as they did the islands to the south and east. Whether for this or other reasons, the British East India Company did establish a free port at Penang, which they occupied in 1786 by agreeing to pay a rental each year to the ruler of Kedah. Trade at the new port grew at the expense of Dutch Malacca and flourished even more after the British, in 1795, took over Malacca, ostensibly to prevent it from falling into French hands.

At the end of the Napoleonic wars in 1814, Malacca was returned to the Dutch. Soon thereafter, in 1819, Raffles founded Singapore. By the Anglo-Dutch Treaty of 1824, the Dutch finally ceded Malacca to the British, acknowledged Singapore as a British possession, and recognized the British sphere of influence in Malaya. The British were thus established at Penang in the northwest, at Malacca on the Strait, and at Singapore at the eastern entrance to the Strait. They in their turn, by the Treaty, recognized Dutch influence in Java and certain other areas in the Archipelago. In the hundred years following, the rest of Malaya came under British domination and administration.

As time went on, the importance and value of Singapore as a port was recognized. Growing British economic involvement in Malay territories gave rise to the necessity for greater political involvement.

Some note should be taken of the affairs of the East India Company in the northern states. Here the Siamese were a factor. Already involved in Perak, the Siamese overran Kedah in 1821. They retained control of this state, but at British insistence recognized the independence of Perak and Selangor. An Anglo-Siamese Treaty of 1826 limited Siamese control to the far northern provinces of Kedah, Perlis, Kelantan and Trenggnau. The treaty arrangements as to Siamese-British relations in the area continued to the end of the century.

At about this same time Penang, Malacca and Singapore were combined for purposes of administration as the Straits Settlements Presidency.

In the years that followed the Malay states witnessed periods of political unrest and civil disturbances. The Straits became a residency under the Presidency of Bengal. East India Company administration was relatively disinterested, and the Settlements were used as a place to which convicts were sent. Many Chinese migrated to the Settlements and to the tin mines in Selangor and elsewhere. Various Chinese factions were frequently in conflict and this had an unsettling effect on British trade in Penang, Singapore and other areas.

The states under Siamese domination in the north were relatively peaceful, although there were frequent intrigues on the part of the sultans and the Siamese. On one occasion the British bombarded Trengganu to frustrate Siamese political ambitions in that state (1862). Elsewhere on the peninsula, by mid-century, the situation was worse. There were civil wars and other disturbances in both Johore and Pahang, in spite of British efforts in support of the ruling sultans. The western Malay states, Perak, Selangor and Sungei Ujong, were also torn by internal strife, but here the problem arose from the large influx of Chinese, the turbulent growth of tin mining and a gradual disintegration of the sultans' authority.

The stage was set for more direct intervention by the British. The impetus for such action came not from London, however, but rather from elements in Malaya. It must be recalled that the East India Company, in the first place, was interested in trade profits rather than in governing vast areas. The function of government or administration was a burden assumed only to secure and maintain profitable trade relations. When the Company lost its monopoly of the China trade in the 1830's it was ill-disposed to disgorge huge sums for the governance of its territories. The least possible effort and expense was devoted to the administration and defense of the Settlements, for example. Nor when the Straits petitioned Parliament in 1858 for direct rule by the crown was the British government much inclined to assume the costly burden of administration of these distant colonies. Non-intervention was the policy in London despite the pleas of European and Chinese merchants for British-imposed stability in the area.

In the 1860's and 1870's the situation had so far deteriorated, what with renewed civil wars and the disintegration of the authority of the sultans in several states, that Britain was forced to take action. The Straits Settlements became a crown colony in 1867, and moves were initiated to install British residents in several of the Malay states. This strategy, it was hoped, would restore peaceful conditions without committing the British government to further and costly intervention. However desirable the objective, further commitments there were, although at the turn of the century British relations with the several states were decidedly disparate and there then existed no definitive plan for future action. From the establishment of the residents in the several states to the Federation of Malaysia spans but half a century; but the path pursued had many windings.

In the 1860's the powers of the sultans began to be exercised increasingly by the aristocratic officeholders of their courts. These officers ruled and taxed their districts with less and less reference to the ruling sultan. Tax receipts often didn't get much further than the district officer. There was no effective control by the central governments in the states to curb civil disorders when they arose. In mid-century, tin was discovered in the west, and the Chinese mining camps that sprang up to take out this new source of wealth were often the scene of bloody disputes over mining claims and water rights.

Turbulent conditions in the mining industry, the deterioration of the sultans' ability to control their peoples, Indian neglect of the Straits Settlements, civil disorders — all combined to unsettle trade in the area. Although the Straits Settlements were removed from Indian administration in 1867, and made a Crown Colony under direct control of the Colonial Office in London, this was not enough. The merchant class voiced repeated demands for more stable conditions. The British were faced with the necessity for further action.

One aspect of the problem centered around the Chinese. The Chinese secret societies were frequently the source of outbreaks of violence. Immigrant Chinese laborers arriving for work in the tin mines joined one or another of these societies. While such associations for the mutual benefit of the members served a useful purpose, they were also often the instruments by which the newly arrived were exploited. Too, the societies often clashed over mining rights and these outbreaks in the 1860's and 1870's resulted in sympathetic outbreaks of rioting in the Settlements' towns. The societies were not finally outlawed until 1889.

Earlier a Chinese Protectorate had been established (1877) to ameliorate the conditions to which the Chinese laborer was exposed. It sought to prevent exploitation by the employer, who was often also an office-holder in the secret society, and the unhealthful and crowded conditions existing in the labor depots.

In an effort to end civil disorders and encourage more effective government in the area, British residents were installed in Perak, Selangor, Negri Sembilan and Pahang. Except in matters of religion and custom, the rulers of these states had to accept their "advice." The residents, in actual effect, controlled the government.

In 1895 the rulers of the four states agreed to a federal arrangement and the administration of the resulting union was under the watchful care of a resident-general in Kuala Lumpur. These were the so-called Federated Malay States.

Although Kedah, Kelantan, Perlis and Trenggau in the north had long been under Siam's domination, in 1902 the Siamese agreed that their advisers to the states might be British officers. By 1909 the Siamese were out, and the British were in. Thenceforth the states were regarded as a part of British Malaya, and in due course each state had its British adviser or agent. In the south the Sultan of Johore also accepted a British adviser.

The establishment of State Councils in 1877, with representatives of the British administration, the Malay rulers and the Chinese community, represented a first, small step toward the eventual evolution of representative government and the acceptance by the Malay sultans of non-Malayans as their subjects. After the federation of Perak, Selangor, Negri Sembilan and Pahang in 1895 and the creation of a strong federal executive, these Councils lost much of their usefulness.

A Federal Council for the federated states was instituted in 1909 with the active participation of the four Malay rulers in an effort to restore to the latter more active direction of the affairs of state and to counter widespread criticism by the Malays that their rulers had been shorn of their rights and power. While it failed in this respect, the Council was the first public body with representatives from all four Malay states — another small step in the forging of a united Malaya. This problem of decentralization, i.e. of restoring greater power to the state governments, continued up to the beginning of World War II.

In the south, the State of Johore was under the strong rule of a wise sultan who ascended the throne in 1895 and reigned for some 60 years. Johore was influenced by the British, but it was not controlled by them. In the four unfederated northern states, there had not been the breakdown in governmental authority and the Malay governments managed to cope adequately with administrative affairs so that the British advisers had neither opportunity nor need to assume the measure of control they exerted in the federated states. For the very reason that the northern states remained unfederated, there was no problem of undue centralization of authority in a federal executive.

By the outbreak of World War I, British influence had been firmly established in each of the states on the peninsula. The nature of the relationship with individual states varied. Penang, Malacca and Singapore formed a crown colony. In the Federated Malay States the residents, under the resident-general in K. L., were virtually in control of government although the native rulers still retained their titles and positions. In the unfederated states the advisers exercised much the same control over government as the residents, but they observed their status as "advisers" in a more formal way so that the "ruling" sultans appeared to have lost fewer of their traditional prerogatives.

As British control of the federated states became increasingly centralized in the resident-general, dissatisfaction among the Malays over this trend became more vocal. Some effort was accordingly made in the years prior to World War I to restore some of the powers of the sultans. A Federal Council, already mentioned, which included the sultans was set up, but no practical decentralization of governmental power resulted. British concern was focused not here, but on the confrontation between the Allied and Central Powers on the European continent. This problem of decentralization was again considered in the early 1920's.

There were differences of opinion within the Malay states themselves as to a proper course of action. Trading interests and the plantation owners took no issue with a strong central government and favored its continuance. Others favored prompt decentralization. Underlying was the basic question as to whether a united, self-governing state should be created or the numerous, small individual states preserved. Between the world wars British official policy reflected the latter alternative.

During the 1930's the Malays developed a considerable political awareness. Numerous politico-cultural associations were formed. These groups generally supported the regime, but some, the Union of Malay Youths, for example, took a radical position. A Malayan Communist Party was also active. The Indian associations, primarily concerned with cultural matters, were not politically oriented.

In spite of benevolent British rule and substantial economic growth, Malaya was anything but a unified political entity when World War II came to the Far East. Its constituent communities had little or no feeling of loyalty to Malaya as such, and the notion of a Malayan "nation" was completely lacking.

The Japanese invaded the peninsula on the day following Pearl Harbor. With her forces largely committed in Europe and in defence of her interests in India and the Middle East, Britain had little manpower to spare for the defense of Malaya. By mid-February 1941, the peninsula and "Fortress Singapore" were in Japanese hands.

The British regime collapsed and efforts at a military defense of Malaya failed. Malayans took little part in military operations, although throughout the war years there were guerrilla bands operating in the jungles and other resistance groups. British officers were parachuted in to assist the guerrillas in the sabotage of Japanese communications. By 1945 the guerrillas were at a strength of about 7,000, but it was not until the issue was decided elsewhere that Malaya was liberated.

During the Japanese occupation Malaya was ruled as a colony by senior officers who functioned as military governors.

To deny to the Japanese war effort the Malaysian output of tin, there had been extensive destruction of mining equipment and machinery as the British withdrew. The export market for rubber had ceased to exist. Both the tin and rubber industries virtually collapsed. Rice production fell and no shipping was available to import supplies. The Japanese printed an ample supply of currency, but in the absence of a supply of goods, the money had little value. Inflation was rampant. Education was disrupted and social services disorganized.

The Japanese regime in Malaysia collapsed in August 1945, and the British were able to reestablish an administration a month later. The Japanese had not, as elsewhere, encouraged a Malayan nationalist movement. The four northern states had been transferred to

Thailand in 1943. At the close of the war it appeared that the future of the rest of the area would be as a part of a greater Indonesia. It was not, in fact, included when the Republic of Indonesia was established.

After the Japanese surrendered, the British returned. Pre-war policy which had favored maintaining the integrity of the sultans and the individual states was reversed. The aim now was for a unification of the states, a self-governing united Malaya within the framework of the Commonwealth.

From September 1945 until April 1946, Malaya was governed by a British Military Administration. The tasks facing this administration and the succeeding civil government were formidable. There was a severe food shortage, unemployment, a currency without value, sporadic looting, a demoralized police force and civil disorders between Malays and Chinese. Order was first established in the towns. Then police in the country districts were reorganized, placed under British officers, and steps initiated to get the economy running again.

Following British defeat in Malaya in 1942, the Colonial Office had addressed itself to the problem of what form a post-war government should take in Malaya. The military rule immediately following the cessation of hostilities afforded a brief period during which steps aimed at unification could be implemented. If action toward this end could be taken quickly enough, the Malay rulers might not be able to focus their objections in this period of uncertainty. In October 1945 the new policy was announced. Penang, Malacca and the nine Malay states (Singapore was excluded) were to be joined in a Malay Union. According to the plan, individual Malay rulers were to cede their sovereign rights to the British Crown. The special position of the Malay community would not be perpetuated in the new order of things. Malays, Chinese and Indians would all be eligible for citizenship if otherwise qualified.

A British emmissary late in 1945 negotiated new agreements with the Malay rulers which vested ultimate jurisdiction over their territories in the British Crown. A Malayan Union was formed and a Governor-General appointed. Singapore remained outside the Union as a crown colony. The arrangement was hastily pushed through. The native rulers were given no time for consultation among themselves, nor for consideration by the State Councils.

Malay public opinion was strong in protest, from the very outset, against the manner in which the unification had been brought about. Early in 1946 a United Malay Nationalist Organization was founded and served as the sounding board of protest against the new constitution. Malay objection was obvious from the refusal of the Malay rulers to attend the inauguration of the first Governor of the Union.

Further discussions were then held among the British, the sultans, and representatives of the UMNO, and a new plan was devised for a Federation of Malaya. A British High Commissioner would govern in the names of the British Crown *and* the Malay rulers. To a limited extent, Malay primacy in the Federation was restored.

A committee was formed with both Asian and British members, and in due course it recommended a federation of states under a high commissioner and an executive council. Such a federation came into being in 1948, under an arrangement by which the individual states retained significant powers.

This looser federation was Malay-led and dissatisfaction on the part of the considerable Chinese populace provided a background for a Communist-led insurrection conducted along lines later to become familiar in Vietnam. The rebellion was put down by the British, but as the result of these trials an enhanced nationalistic feeling emerged in Malaya. Before tracing the sequence of events by which the new Federation gained independence and the subsequent founding of the state of Malaysia, some account must be given of this so-called "Emergency" period.

Communism came to Malaya in the 1920's. It gained some followers because the Communists had supported the Chinese national movement of the Kuomintang. Similarly, the party benefited from an enhanced patriotic feeling among the Malayan Chinese when the Japanese attacked mainland China in 1937. During the Japanese occupation of Malaya it was the Communists who led the resistance movement among the Chinese.

Communism in Malaya was Chinese. In the earliest period of World War II, immediately after the Japanese invasion, the Malayan Communist Party cooperated with the government in resisting the common enemy. However much the Communists wanted to see the British out of Malaya, the first task was the expulsion of the Japanese. They took a major role in the Malayan Peoples Anti-Japanese Army, a guerrilla formation which to the end of the war harrassed the invaders, though with no decisive result. It was disbanded in December 1945.

At the end of the war the Party was well organized and in the two or three years after the cessation of hostilities reached its apex of power. This was accomplished in large measure by penetration and control of the trades unions. Their efforts to infiltrate the unions were facilitated by the high cost of rice and other necessaries, and they were relatively successful. A one-day general strike was called in January 1946. Other strikes followed. Thousands of workers were idled and unrest was rampant throughout the labor force. In 1947 the Communists may well have possessed the power to totally disrupt, if not destroy, the Malayan economy. At the same time, the government took strong measures to curb disruptive union activity, passed trade union legislation to bring these abuses under control, and the economy improved. The Party leadership faced a crisis. Faced with internal dissension and defections, the Party leaders moved toward open revolt as a means of preserving their own position within the Party.

In the 1946-48 period the MCP also made an effort for alignment with other political movements which opposed the Anglo-Malay coalition and spoke out against the proposed constitution of the Federation. For a time these opposition parties appeared to be making headway. When the Federation of Malaya (as successor to the Malay Union) became a fact in February 1948, however, the alliance of these parties (including several Communist organizations) with the Malayan Democratic Union and the Malay Nationalist Party finally broke up. From this confused period one party with substantial support from all sections of the Malay community did emerge — the United Malay National Organisation.

At the outset of the Communist revolt in 1948 there were stores of weapons still hidden in the jungles from wartime. These arms had been airlifted during the war to the MPAJA by the British from India and Ceylon. There was also a hard core of "old comrades" of the MPAJA forces, many of whom had demobilized most reluctantly and were now disposed to fight the British and the new order.

The grand strategy of the insurrection movement was to paralyze the economy. The objective explains Communist interest in infiltrating the unions. Further dislocation was to be brought about by armed attacks on the plantations and mines. As Communist control was established, "liberated areas" were to be created, and then the party leadership envisaged a great popular uprising which would bring these areas together and finally result in the "liberation" of the entire country.

The revolt was heralded by the brutal murder of three plantation managers in Perak in June 1948. In the course of the insurrection, ten per cent of the planters in Malaya met a similar fate, along with hundreds of mining managers and other mining personnel – even common laborers – who were assassinated, ambushed or otherwise killed.

In what is now, since Vietnam, a familiar pattern of Communist guerrilla warfare, small groups operated in and out of the jungle – against police outposts, remote Malay villages, to ambush and kill officials, plantation managers, to steal rubber. Throughout it was a hit and run war. The terrorists would strike and then quickly vanish into the jungle. Ferreting out these small bands was a tedious and time-consuming task. They defended no fixed territory. They were extremely mobile. They took the struggle with them as they moved. Against a probable total of no more than 8,000 terrorists the government committed 40,000 regulars and 70,000 police plus supporting arms and thousands of village militia, the "home guards." When security forces did come up against a guerrilla band, the latter quickly broke contact and fled into the jungle depths, only to appear in another place the next day or next week.

The government responded quickly and wisely to the Communist effort. To insure against a breakdown of the economy, substantial security forces were committed to protect such installations as were vital to its continuing function. Emergency regulations were placed into effect. Several thousand Chinese, actual or potential supporters of the rebels, were deported. Most significantly, the centers of population were made secure from the Communist terror. Thousands of Chinese "squatters" were moved from their small landholdings into resettlement areas from which they could no longer serve as a source of food supply for the guerrillas. In past times of unemployment, in order to survive, large numbers of Chinese laborers simply went off to the edges of the jungle, cleared land and started to grow their own food. They were "squatters" because at best the only title to the land they worked was a temporary occupation license, and usually they had no title at all.

In the early fifties the struggle continued, but the high water mark of Communistic successes was reached in 1952. The tide was turning.

Following the ambush death of Sir Henry Gurney, the high commissioner, late in 1951, a new commissioner and operations director was appointed — General Sir Gerald Templer. His firm action and unbounded energy kept the pressure on the Communists while they were at the same time forced to an agonizing reappraisal of their failure to win over the masses. They were thenceforth increasingly on the defensive. In a fruitless effort to gain wider popular support the random terrorism against the civilian population decreased. The guerrillas withdrew deep into the jungle where they sought to reorganize and set up cultivation areas to provide a food supply.

Gradually the situation was mastered. The terrorists, themselves masters of ambush, were in turn ambushed when they came out for supplies. Food supplies were cut off when the squatters were relocated in protected compounds — the so-called "new villages." Security forces concentrated their efforts in limited, selected areas and the guerrillas were rooted out man by man over a period of weeks or months. New areas were selected and the process repeated, until finally the remnants of the Communist forces — only a few hundred men — were pushed up into the northern area bordering Thailand.

The government met with MCP leaders in late 1955. Having failed thus far in their revolt, the latter had the audacity to ask that their party be legalized and permitted to engage in "normal" policital activity. When sternly rebuffed, they went back to fighting in desultory fashion, now with little hope of victory. There was no formal "end" to the insurrection. With the MCP leaders fugitives in the deep jungle and what remained of the terrorist bands localized in the north, the threat simply died away, and the "Emergency" declared to be ended in mid-1960.

While the Communists pursued their exercise in futility, Malaya had become independent. The MCP was discredited and without political influence in the life of the new nation.

Now to return to the sequence of events by which the Federation of Malaya gained independence. These events transpired during the years 1948 to 1957.

The Federation of Malaya came into being on February 1, 1948. Under the constitution, the Federal Legislative Council was appointive rather than elective. A Federal Executive Council was made up of ministrial advisers to the High Commissioner. The executive was not responsible to the legislature, but the latter held the purse strings so that in a very real sence the executive governed only with the consent of the legislators. There were numerous other checks and balances.

In due course, as the nation moved toward independence, election replaced nomination as the means of filling the legislature, and a cabinet whose ministers were responsible to the legislature replaced the executive council.

Political parties, of which the United Malay National Organization was most prominent, assumed a new and important role in determining the composition of government. The UMNO had fought hard and successfully against the Malayan Union and for the rights of their rulers and the Malays in government. The Malay Chinese Association (MCA) was dedicated to preserving the interests of the Chinese community. The Indian community had its own group, the Malayan Indian Congress (MIC). A new party, the Independence of Malaya Party, was organized late in 1951 under the leadership of a former president of the UMNO.

It was at this time that Tunku Abdul Rahman, a man who was to play an important role both before and after independence, became president of the UMNO. The next year, intent upon defeating IMP candidates in the Kuala Lumpur municipal elections, the UMNO and MCA formed a coalition. This "Alliance" was curious in that the period was marked by Sino-Malay disagreement on many issues, on citizenship in particular. Without citizenship Malayan Chinese had no vote. For MCA support, the UMNO went along with new rules which gave the franchise to about half of the Chinese in the Federation. In spite of these tensions, the Alliance endured, won a victory in the elections in the federal capital and joined forces to urge elections for state and federal councils. In early 1954 the cause was won; the government announced elections to be held in 1955. The Alliance won by a landslide in the federal council elections in July — 51 of 52 seats! And the party platform was little more than the promise of self-government and independence as soon as possible. Rahman took office as Chief Minister.

Early in the following year (1956) Rahman and several of his ministers went to London to press for full independence. There was surprisingly little resistance to their demands, and August 1957 was set as the date. A commission was promptly appointed to draft the outline for a new constitution for an independent Federation. As finally adopted, this basic law provided for a supreme head of state, selected by and from among the rulers of the Malay states for a 5-year term; a cabinet of ministers selected from the majority party in the federal council; a bicameral federal legislature (the lower house entirely elective); and a judiciary.

Penang and Malacca, now no longer under the Crown, joined the nine Malay States as constituent members of the Federation, which elected to remain within the Commonwealth of Nations.

Independence was proclaimed on August 31, 1957. All of this was brought about in just two years — a monumental achievement for which much credit must be given to the Alliance party and to Tunku Abdul Rahman, president of the UMNO and first Prime Minister of the Federation of Malaya.

The question of extending the Federation to embrace additional states was raised at least as early as 1961, and the status of Singapore was to a considerable extent central to the issue. It will be recalled that three-fourths of the population of Singapore is Chinese and the primary fear of the Federation government was that if Singapore were to be merged into a new and larger Malaysia, Malay political supremacy would be lost. The powerful Alliance party had not favored an association with Singapore up to this point. Singapore posed a threat to inter-communal harmony in Malaya because of its traditional sympathy with Chinese nationalistic aims.

On the other hand, the increasingly leftist governments and even the threat of a Communist takeover made it appear that the security of Malaya might be better served with Singapore inside the Federation rather than remaining as a threat outside it. There were, of course, many other considerations. One way of counterbalancing the entry of Singapore might have been the merger as well of Sarawak and North Borneo (Sabah). This, in fact, is what happened.

The Singapore electorate favored a merger as evidenced by the results of a referendum. A joint British-Malayan commission appointed to investigate the matter recommended the merger of Sarawak and Sabah and a UN team of investigators confirmed that a majority of the people of the two states favored federation with Malaya. A third state in Borneo, Brunei, declined to join. Singapore bargained skillfully and gained a considerable measure of local autonomy, though at the cost of returning fewer representatives to the federal parliament than the population ratio justified.

Under the Malaysia Agreement, concluded in London on July 9, 1963, the United Kingdom agreed to transfer sovereignty over Singapore, Sarawak and North Borneo (Sabah) to the new Malaysian Federation. The new Federation of Malaysia was proclaimed on September 16, 1963. In West Malaysia there were the former states of the Federation of Malaya (Johore, Kedah, Kelantan, Malacca, Negri Sembilan, Pahang, Penang and Province Wellesley, Perak, Perlis, Selangor, Trengganu) plus Singapore; in East Malaysia the two states, Sarawak and Sabah.

The structure of government generally followed the pattern of the Federation: a supreme head of state elected by the hereditary rulers of the nine Malay states from among their number; a parliament with members of the lower house elected for 5-year terms, and members of the senate appointed or elected for 6-year terms by the state legislatures. Supreme judicial authority rests with the High Courts of West and East Malaysia. Individual member states each have an elected legislature and a chief minister and executive council. Kuala Lumpur is the capital of the Federation.

Indonesian opposition to the formation of Malaysia led to a protracted period of "confrontation" between the two nations, a rupture in diplomatic relations between Malaysia and both Indonesia and the Philippines (the latter had advanced claims to Sabah), and sporadic raids by Indonesian "volunteers" into Malaysian territory on Borneo and even into Malaya itself. By mid-1966 the confrontation had run out of steam. Sukarno was on the way out, the Indonesian Communist Party had been crushed, and the generals who took power in Indonesia were not inclined to continue the unsuccessful campaign against their northern neighbor. An agreement concluded between the two powers in 1966 provided for an end to the struggle and a resumption of diplomatic relations.

The brief historical notes, by way of background, which are supplied here have obviously omitted any detailed reference to East Malaysia. This has been the case largely because the writer's travels were only on the peninsula, and because the broad history of trade in the region — which had such a powerful influence in determining political and economic patterns — centers on the peninsular ports and Singapore.

Across Malaysia by Rail

Malaysia is accessible by any of several means of transportation.

The nation's airline, Malaysian Airline System, flys to Bangkok, Hong Kong, Taipei, Tokyo, Djakarta, Singapore and elsewhere in Southeast Asia, with additional routes projected to London, Manila and Sydney. Both Singapore Airlines and Thai International come into Kuala Lumpur, as do nearly 20 other international carriers. MAS has a well-developed domestic service as well.

It is also possible to tour the country by auto. The Asian Highway, which stretches from Singapore to the northern border of Thailand, crosses Malaysia, and there are numerous inter-city express bus services.

For the traveler who wants a close look at the countryside from the air-conditioned comfort of a railway car, the Malayan Railway provides first-class service on north and south bound day express trains from Kuala Lumpur. These lines go to Butterworth and Singapore. Air-conditioned compartments and sleeping berths are available on the night expresses. At Butterworth (opposite Penang Island) there is a connection with the international express to and from Bangkok.

Padang Besar is on the Thai-Malaysian border, and the traveler entering the country from the north leaves the train briefly here for customs and immigration formalities. Although not actually in sight of the sea, the railroad follows the western coastline to Alor Star (Kedah) and Butterworth (Prai). There are long stretches of dense vegetation punctuated by flat areas where rice is under cultivation. Now and again one catches sight of a mosque and minaret. Malaysia is a Muslim country.

The houses along the river in Alor Star are out of a picture book. There are thatch roofs, small boats tied up virtually at the front door, women washing and cooking, and small children splashing about in the water. On toward Sungei Patani there are miles of rice fields with rice full grown against a backdrop of mountains off to the east. In this area the country seems quite prosperous. The farmers' houses are well built, the highways well maintained and a general atmosphere of prosperity.

When harvested the rice fields present a brown stubble 8 or 10 inches above the ground, or above the water as the case may be. Where harvesting is in progress the field hands thrash a bundle of rice against a large basket with a sort of fabric enclosure on three sides to prevent loss of the golden grains.

Butterworth is on the mainland opposite the Island of Penang,

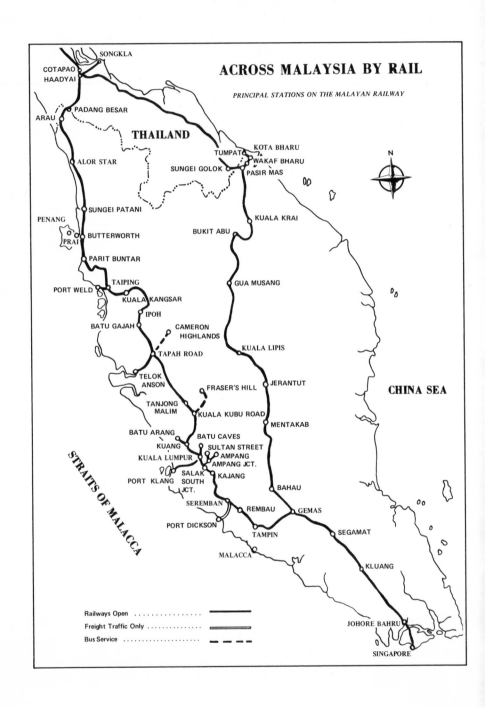

ACROSS MALAYSIA BY RAIL

PRINCIPAL STATIONS ON THE MALAYAN RAILWAY

SONGKLA
COTAPAO
HAADYAI
PADANG BESAR
ARAU
THAILAND
ALOR STAR
KOTA BHARU
TUMPAT
WAKAF BHARU
SUNGEI GOLOK
PASIR MAS
SUNGEI PATANI
PENANG
KUALA KRAI
BUKIT ABU
BUTTERWORTH
PRAI
PARIT BUNTAR
TAIPING
GUA MUSANG
PORT WELD
KUALA KANGSAR
IPOH
BATU GAJAH
CAMERON HIGHLANDS
KUALA LIPIS
TAPAH ROAD
TELOK ANSON
FRASER'S HILL
JERANTUT
CHINA SEA
TANJONG MALIM
KUALA KUBU ROAD
MENTAKAB
BATU ARANG
BATU CAVES
KUANG
SULTAN STREET
KUALA LUMPUR
AMPANG
AMPANG JCT.
SALAK SOUTH
PORT KLANG
KAJANG
JCT.
BAHAU
SEREMBAN
REMBAU
GEMAS
PORT DICKSON
TAMPIN
SEGAMAT
MALACCA
KLUANG
STRAITS OF MALACCA
JOHORE BAHRU
SINGAPORE

N

Railways Open . . . .
Freight Traffic Only . . . .
Bus Service . . . .

Kuala Lumpur's Moorish-style Railway Station

National Mosque in Kuala Lumpur

Malaysian Parliament House

National Monument in the Lake Gardens

Night View of National Monument

Sultan Abu Bakar Mosque in Johore

Malacca River View

St. John's Hill in Malacca

Malaysian Rubber Plantation

Rubber Tapper at Work

Tin Dredge

"Palong" or Gravel Pump Mining

Penang's Funicular Railway

which is two miles offshore and readily accessible by ferry boats which depart every few minutes from the station complex. Penang has been called "the Pearl of the Orient." Rightly so. Waving palm trees, powdery beaches and clear blue waters offer a prospect of scenic splendor. Crossing over from the mainland as dusk fades into night the boat glides almost silently into the natural harbor of the city of Georgetown, which is situated on the coastal plain at the northeast corner of the island. In the background the high hills in the center of the island are backlighted by a tropical moon, and the lights on shore blink a message of welcome and adventure.

It was here that Captain Francis Light, of the British East India Company, came in 1786. The Island was almost uninhabited, though now and then used as a refuge by Indian Ocean pirates. On a return visit, Light negotiated with the Sultan of Kedah for the lease of the island as a site for a Company trading post. He was successful and took formal possession of Penang in August 1786. It remained a British colony from that date until it became a part of independent Malaysia in 1957.

The first British settlement in the Straits of Malacca, it became an important trading center. Chinese, Indians, Arabs and others found a home here along with the indigenous Malays. The multi-racial population is reflected by the different religious institutions and houses of worship to be found here. In the center of Georgetown, for example, there are the Kapitan Kling Mosque, which is one of Malaysia's oldest and largest, and St. George's Church, the oldest Anglican church in the country. The largest Buddhist temple in Malaysia is not far away on the lower slopes of Penang Hill. This is the Ayer Itam (Kek Lok Si) Temple. Elsewhere on the island there are several Chinese temples, including the curious Snake Temple where live snakes curl among the carvings, prayer tables and joss stick stands.

An ascent to the top of 2,270-foot Penang Hill can be made by funicular railway. There is a lovely panorama view of the landscape, seacoast and ocean from the peak.

Returning to the mainland, the night express leaves Butterworth in the early evening, and passing through Taiping, Ipoh and Tapah Road, reaches Kuala Lumpur early the next morning.

Kuala Lumpu (usually called simply "K. L."), now a federal district, is the nation's capital. In the immediate area round the city there are many rubber plantations, tin mines and an imposing mountain range.

For the visitor arriving by train, the first impression of K. L. may well be that made by the railroad station. Impressive it is. It is a very large structure in the Moorish style and looks like it should be a sultan's palace. Just opposite is the Masjid Negara (National Mosque) which is of modern Moorish design and placed like a jewel in a setting of green lawns and ornamental pools. From the top of its slender minaret one can view the entire city.

The main dome is in the shape of an 18-point star to represent the thirteen states of Malaysia and the five Pillars of Islam. There are many smaller domes, much like those of the Great Mosque in Mecca.

The city was founded in 1857 by Chinese miners who came up the Klang River in search of tin. When they reached the confluence of the Klang and Gomback Rivers, they came ashore and continued their search overland. Kuala Lumpur was established as a trading post for workers in the tin mines in the Klang River basin. From this humble beginning it has grown to a city of 750,000 people. Modern office buildings and luxury hotels contrast with Moorish-style government buildings, mosques and older 19th century structures. The numerous mosques and Moorish architecture impart a Middle-Eastern atmosphere that is unique in the Far East.

One of the most picturesque of the moorish-style structures is the Old Secretariat Building with its great central clock tower. It occupies the eastern side of the Padang in the city center. Masjid Jame (the Jame Mosque) is close by at the junction of the two rivers. It is the oldest mosque in the city and is situated in a garden of palm trees.

The Lake Gardens, with woodland beauty and cool waters, provide welcome open space in the city. Parliament House and an adjoining block of government offices are centrally located in the Gardens and the National Monument is also here. The latter was designed by Felix de Welden, who also created the Iwo Jima Memorial in Washington. The Monument consists of seven huge figures cast in bronze and mounted on a pedestal of granite — a memorial to those who fought and died in action against the Communists during the 12-year emergency period (1948-1960). The National Museum, at the edge of the Lake Gardens, offers dramatic exhibits of Malaysia's cultural heritage, history, crafts, traditions and customs.

The National Art Gallery in Tunku Abdul Rahman Hall, on Jalan Ampang, houses a fine collection of works by Malaysian artists.

A short drive outside the city to the north brings the visitor past several rubber plantations. In the morning hours the tappers are busy at work tapping the trees for latex. Also, on Klang Road, one can observe tin dredging. One of the largest dredge mines in the world is about seven miles north of the city, and the open-cast mine near Sungei Besi is the world's largest. At about the eighth mile are the Batu Caves. These vast caverns in an outcrop of limestone are held to be sacred by Malaysia's Hindu community. In late January each year Hindu pilgrims make their way here to honor the deity Lord Subramanian. Still further, along the Ipoh Road, there is a stretch of virgin jungle in relatively hilly country. This is Templer Park. A network of jungle paths and cascading streams cross the park, and there is an excellent opportunity here to study at close hand the many species of Malaysian flora and fauna.

Leaving Kuala Lumpur to resume the journey southward, the express train passes through Seremban, Tampin, Gemas and on to Johore Bahru.

Although it is not on the rail line, historic old Malacca can be visited easily enough by air or bus and the traveler will find much of interest. To begin with, it is the oldest town in Malaysia and the site of the capital of the old Malaccan Sultanate. Here the Portuguese captain Alfonso d'Albuquerque came in 1511. A little more than a century later the Dutch ousted the Portuguese and remained for a century and a half until they, in their turn, made way for the British. Each era is marked by surviving relics and picturesque buildings. The town has a quaint, almost medieval, charm all its own.

Malacca was once the greatest city in Southeast Asia. From here cargoes of tin, ivory, pepper and other spices, silks and even gold, were shipped westward.

The Chinese were trading with Malacca as early as the time of the Ming Emperor Yung Lo, long before Columbus discovered America. As trade flourished many Chinese came to live here, and their presence is still marked by the existence of several old temples and landmarks. The Cheng Hoon Teng Temple is the oldest Chinese temple in Malaysia. Bukit China ("Chinese Hill") rises just behind another temple, the Poh San Teng. It was upon this hill, centuries ago, that a Ming Emperor's daughter made her residence as wife of the Malacca Sultan. Some very ancient Chinese relics are to be seen on Bukit China as well as the graves of some early Chinese dignitaries.

The Sultan's Well, at the foot of the hill, is said to date back to the founding of Malacca in the 13th century.

During the Portuguese period there were, within the city walls, two fine palaces and a castle, several churches and a great hall for the Portuguese Council of State. Of the once formidable fortress that was raised here only the gateway of Porto De Santiago is to be seen. The rest of the structure was torn down by the British early in the last century. The remains of one of the early Portuguese churches, St. Paul's, can be seen atop Residency Hill. Reared first as a chapel, in 1521, it was used by St. Francis Xavier when he visited Malacca. The Saint died here and his body was interred in St. Paul's until it was later removed to Goa. Although built nearly two centuries later, the Church of St. Peter in Jalan Bendahara also reflects the ages-old influence of the Portuguese period of domination. It is now the Church of the Portuguese Mission. Its architecture is interesting as an admixture of eastern and western styles.

The period of Dutch occupation is marked by a number of notable churches and other buildings. The oldest is the Stadthuys, built sometime in the middle of the 17th century. It presently houses government offices, and its continuous use for more than two centuries is proof of the skill and permanence with which it was constructed. Its massive walls, heavy doors and window frames seem to give promise that it may well be in use for another century or two. Christ Church, built a century later in 1753, is a splendid example of Dutch architecture. Its pink bricks were brought by sea all the way from Zeeland, and its fine louvre windows, wooden doors and long interior ceiling beams are especially noteworthy. A painting of "The Last Supper" decorates the marble altar. The Church is now Anglican, but a number of antique silver vessels with the Dutch coat-of-arms are still to be seen.

Not to be overlooked is the Tranquerah Mosque. It is of Sumatran design and contains the tomb of the Johore Sultan who ceded Singapore to Sir Stamford Raffles in 1819.

The capital of the State of Johore is Johore Bahru, overlooking the Johore Strait which separates Malaysia from Singapore. The state is the southernmost in Malaysia, heavily forested with large areas of swampland. Rice culture is not important, but there are a million acres in rubber. Numerous plantations produce palm oil, and pineapples are grown. Most of the bauxite produced in the country comes from southwest Johore, and there is some iron mining.

Johore Bahru is closely allied to Singapore in an economic sense. Much of the farm produce of the area goes to Singapore markets, and the city serves as the outlet for Malaysian goods moving into Singapore's port area for further shipment. All Malaysian transport has to cross the causeway, by rail or highway, to reach the island. The Strait, at the causeway, is only a half-mile wide.

There are a number of government buildings to be seen in the city itself. The State Secretariat Building is impressive with its tall square tower reminiscent of an oversized old Norman keep. A number of the others are of the most modern design.

The Istana or official residence of the Sultan of Johore is at the edge of the city. Although the Sultan and his family do not now live here, it is the site of official state functions. It was actually occupied as a residence by the present Sultan's grandfather. The building is set in beautifully landscaped grounds and a short distance away stands the Sultan Mosque, high up and overlooking the Strait. The muezzin's call to prayer still sounds, through loud speakers, five times a day. A Muslim cemetery and the royal mausoleum are in the vicinity.

Immigration and customs offices are at the entrance to the causeway, and this area is typically congested with autos, motor buses from various parts of southern Malaysia, and trucks — traffic headed into or out of Singapore. The express train coming from Kuala Lumpur also passes over the causeway and terminates at the main railway station in Singapore.

Chapter 5

SINGAPORE –
THE LION CITY

Singapore lies at the extreme southern tip of the Malay peninsula, 85 miles above the equator. An independent republic since it withdrew from the Federation of Malaysia in 1965, the land is separated from the mainland by the Johore Strait. It consists of one main island and 59 smaller ones, with a total area of approximately 225 square miles. Singapore Island is about 26 miles long (east to west) and 14 miles wide (north to south). When the Englishman Raffles arrived in 1819, the island was largely swampland and covered with jungle. As late as 1850 tigers prowled the countryside, but over the years the land was cleared and the wild animals are no more. There is little left of the original forested areas as well. The climate is humid with daytime temperatures ranging around a mean of 82 degrees (F.).

Of the more than two million inhabitants, three-fourths are Chinese. About 300,000 Malays constitute the next largest racial group, and there are Indians, Pakistanis, Eurasians and Europeans. Malay, Mandarin Chinese, Tamil and English are the four official languages. Islam, Buddhism, Confucianism, Taoism and Hinduism are the major faiths, but other religions are represented.

The City of Singapore has the largest port in Southeast Asia, and the fourth largest in the world. There are the deepwater facilities of Keppel Harbour, and much cargo is still unloaded from ships anchored in the roads. Situated astride major air and water routes, the City has become one of the world's major business and shipping centers. Twenty-seven airlines operate services from or through the international airport at Paya Lebar.

Although the island itself produces little rubber, Singapore is an important rubber exporter. Petroleum products and machinery are also major exports. Much of Malaysia's foreign trade, including shipments of rubber and tin, passes through the port to destinations in the United States, the United Kingdom, Japan, Hong Kong and elsewhere. In a recent year more than 36,000 ships entered and cleared the port. Malaysian Railways links the harbor with the mainland via a causeway across Johore Strait.

From its founding Singapore has been a free port, and there were virtually no duties imposed until the 1950's. With the development of industry, some protective duties are now levied, but there are still free trade zones and numerous exemptions from duty apply to goods brought in for processing and re-export.

About half of the island remains under cultivation. Agricultural output includes vegetables, fruit, tapioca, pepper and tobacco, and pigs and poultry are raised. Although rice (padi) is a staple item in the diet, it is no longer grown here. Fishing in the coastal waters is also important.

The government is making an intensive effort to encourage industry and attract foreign investment. Industrial sites have been developed for both light and heavy industry. The largest is the Jurong Industrial Estate with its huge National Iron and Steel Mill. There are more than 450 factories at Jurong. The Economic Development Board offers technical and financial assistance, and new enterprises can secure tax exemptions and other advantages intended to enhance the growth of new industries. The Development Bank in Singapore is prepared to supply substantial equity investment in foreign enterprises coming to the island. Some of the undertakings are huge. A recent joint venture with a Japanese firm, for example, involves the construction of a great petrochemical complex.

The drive for industrialization has increased land values, and some agricultural land-use will eventually give way to the needs of industry. It is primarily because of the success of new industries that gross national product has more than tripled in the past decade.

Historical Background

The earliest "history" of Singapore is largely a matter of tradition. Legend has it that long ago a Palembang prince, Sang Nila Uttama, sought refuge on the island from a storm at sea and landed at Tumasek (the old Malay name for Singapore, meaning "sea town"). He sighted a large animal on the shore which he mistook for a lion and renamed the place *Singapura*. This comes from the Sanskrit words *singa* (lion) and *pura* (city), literally Lion City. He established his rule on the island and the place grew into a trading center of some importance.

In the 11th century A.D. a Chola ruler (Rajendracola Deva, 1016-1044) attacked the island in his drive against the empire of Srivijaya. There may have been an attack by the Javanese late in the 13th century, and in 1377 Javanese Majaphit invaders captured and sacked the place. The site remained settled but was of little importance for many years following. There is also a record of an unsuccessful seige by Siamese warships in the mid-14th century when the island was subjected to the Javanese empire. In 1552 St. Francis Xavier mentions it as a place of shipping and trade.

Any sketch of the political and economic development of the area must take into account the colonial rivalries which existed in the Malay Archipelago from the early 16th century onward. This vast area stretches from Sumatra, directly across the Strait from Singapore, to the Philippine Islands far to the east. Singapore came into being largely because the British sought to carve out a sphere of influence and trade in the area.

The major colonial powers of the West were all attracted to the fabled riches of the Archipelago. The Portuguese came in 1511 and again in 1514. The Spanish came too, and already in 1529, by treaty, these two powers sought to settle their respective spheres of influence. The Dutch came late in the century, first to Sumatra. The Dutch East India Company (incorporated 1602) was destined to play a major role in Indonesia for the next two centuries. By 1608 they had much the best of the Portuguese and were firmly established with their headquarters at Batavia (Djakarta). The early part of the century witnessed intense rivalry between the Dutch and English as well. After the treaty of Westminster in 1674 the British concentrated on their possessions in India while the Dutch had a relatively free hand in the Archipelago. By the mid-18th century the Dutch were in control of Java. Great Britain was determined to prevent a Dutch monopoly of the Malaya trade and of the avenues to trade with China. The opportunity came during the Napoleonic wars. The European Netherlands as well as the Netherland Indies were at that time a part of Napoleon's empire; and Great Britain was at war with Napoleon. What better reason for British action against the Dutch in the Indies? In 1811 the British inflicted a resounding defeat on the Dutch and captured Java. It is at this point that the name Raffles is encountered.

Raffles Founds Singapore

Sir Thomas Stamford Raffles was born in 1781, son of a ship's master engaged in the West Indies trade. Self-educated, since there was no money to provide him with a formal education, Raffles became a clerk at East India House when he was but 14 years of age. The East India Company, founded in the time of Elizabeth I, had a monopoly on East-West trade and exercised governing powers in India.

With Great Britain at war with Napoleon, the Company's directors were concerned to safeguard their trade route to China. Since Pitt's India Bill of 1784, the directors were subject to a government Board of Control in setting broad policy. The French, in effective control of Holland on the European continent, were in possession of the Dutch East Indies, and Calcutta to Canton shipping was vulnerable to French warships. The Company directors and the Board of Control determined to develop and strengthen Penang (Prince of Wales Island) as an intermediate station on the India-China trade route. It was made a Presidency, and when it became necessary to send out additional personnel to implement these plans Raffles was selected as an assistant to the Chief Secretary at Penang. It was in this manner that he left London, in 1805, for the Far East.

He applied himself with such zeal in the discharge of his duties that in less than two years he had become Chief Secretary to the Governor.

He gained a singular grasp of the complex political situation in the region, and as the indirect result of a detailed situation report he prepared on the subject he came to the attention of Lord Minto, then Governor General in India. Following a meeting with Minto, Raffles was appointed the Governor's agent in Malaya, with headquarters in Malacca. His immediate mission was to determine the feasibility of an invasion of Java, which was in French hands. A successful strike there would at once ease the French threat to Calcutta-Canton shipping and contain the Dutch.

The invasion was decided upon, and Minto promoted Raffles to the post of Secretary to the Governor General. The fleet and invading army sailed from Malacca in June 1811 along a route selected by Raffles. Six weeks later the troops were landed on Java in the vicinity of Batavia (modern Djakarta). The French and Dutch forces were routed and Batavia taken. Java was annexed and Raffles appointed to head the British administration which Minto left behind.

For the next several years, until 1816, Raffles governed Java. He managed to enlist the cooperation of the Dutch colonials, parleyed with the native sultans and instituted major reforms in the administration to the dual benefit of the Javanese and his own rule. He faced ·numerous difficulties, however. The costs of administering the annexed territory could not be met locally and were a source of annoyance to the Board and Directors of the East India Company in England. They had not favored annexation in the first place, since it was widely believed that Java would revert to Holland once Napoleon was defeated and peace restored. Too, Minto's term as Governor General ended and with his return to England Raffles could no longer count on his powerful support. Finally, there were difficulties with the army commander in Java who resisted Raffles' civil authority over his actions. The commander went so far as to prefer charges against Raffles with Minto's successor, Lord Moira (later Marquess of Hastings). Although eventually exonerated from these unjust charges, Raffles was recalled from his post and given the Residency (later elevated to a Lieutenant Governorship) of Bencoolen, a not very important British settlement on the south coast of Sumatra.

Before taking up this new charge, Raffles returned to England. He had been in the east for a decade, and the state of his health and his career were most likely to benefit from a stay in England. He was most favorably received. He enjoyed the friendship of Princess Charlotte, daughter of the Prince Regent, was knighted, elected a Fellow of the Royal Society, met George Canning (later to be Prime Minister), was feted by London society and honored by many learned Englishmen who acknowledged his scholarship in far eastern matters. His two-volume *History of Java* was published at this time and was acclaimed as a notable contribution to what was known of the East Indies.

Raffles was convinced that he still had a role to play in the East. Earlier he had tendered to Canning a paper in which he outlined the steps he believed necessary if British interests in the Archipelago were to be secured. One measure he advised was the establishment of another British settlement, this one to be at the eastern end of the Strait of Malacca strategically located to command this vital waterway between the Indian and China seas. Such a settlement, he believed, would be effective in countering Dutch designs on English trade in the area. When he sailed late in 1817 for Bencoolen he had been given certain advisory duties as well as charge of the administration of the settlement in south Sumatra.

He applied himself with diligence to the latter task, established good relations with native chiefs in the surrounding area and made several trips into the interior in furtherance of his natural history research. At the same time he was planning how best to counter Dutch restrictions on trade. He realized that any concrete step in this direction would require the approval and support of Lord Hastings, the Governor General in Calcutta.

A meeting with Hastings was arranged. For a variety of reasons, Hastings was no longer ill-disposed toward the former Lieutenant Governor of Java. He shared Raffles' interest in frustrating Dutch ambitions, affairs in India had been suitably arranged so that he could now devote more time to matters in the east, and, after all, had not Raffles been given favorable recognition by the Prince Regent himself. While Hastings was aware of the growing Dutch threat to the British line of communications to China, the authorities in London demanded that he pursue a policy which would not offend the Dutch or endanger the peace settlement in Europe reached at the end of the Napoleonic wars. He was, however, won over to Raffles' view that a new settlement must immediately be established at the eastern end of the Strait of Malacca. The island of Rhio was in particular mentioned as a likely site in the letter of instructions Raffles received from Hastings.

At Penang, where he was to secure troops for the undertaking, Raffles learned that the Dutch were already on Rhio. He accordingly decided to try Johore, which Hastings had indicated as an alternative.

Raffles' ships reached the island of Singapore on January 28, 1819, and he landed on the day following. He sought out the local chief and offered a rent in exchange for land upon which to found a settlement. The chief could neither accept nor reject the offer. This was the prerogative of the Sultan of Johore, since Singapore Island was a part of that state.

Matters were further complicated by the fact that there was a dispute as to the succession of the rule in Johore. The usurper and brother of the legitimate claimant had been recognized by the Dutch, and he would certainly not have negotiated with the English. Raffles decided to back the claim of the legitimate heir. He managed to bring the latter to Singapore, persuaded him to take the throne and even arranged an appropriate ceremony to mark the event. At the same time a treaty was concluded with the new sultan which granted the right of settlement to the East India Company in exchange for an annual payment.

A Resident was appointed, staff organized, orders issued for the construction of a fort to assure the defense and other details settled as to the conduct of affairs at this newest of British outposts. Thus was Singapore founded, free port, bastion against Dutch aggrandizement, gateway to the Strait of Malacca, and, more than anything else the realization of one man's idea — the belief of Sir Stamford Raffles that this settlement would ensure the continuing growth of British trade and maritime power in the East.

The agreement Raffles concluded in 1819 provided only for permission to establish a settlement, i.e. a trading post of the East India Company, at the mouth of the Singapore River. In 1824 a further treaty ceded the entire island to the Company.

The Dutch, of course, promptly lodged a formal protest with Penang. They based their title to Singapore on the ground that it was a part of Johore, Johore a dependency of Malacca, and Malacca a Dutch possession since it was handed over by the British in 1816. In any event the Dutch expected Hastings to disavow Raffles' action; but this he did not do. It was only after seemingly endless negotiations with the Dutch and protracted discussions in London that the British right to Singapore was established by an Anglo-Dutch treaty in 1824. By this same treaty Malacca was handed back to the British and the area in the Archipelago south of the equator was acknowledged to be Dutch. England's trade routes to China were now secure!

Singapore in the Modern Era

In 1826 the island became part of the Straits Settlements. As the fortunes of the East India Company declined in the 1830's, so did its concern with Singapore. By 1851 Singapore had come under the control of the Governor General of India, and some years later (in

1867) the Straits Settlements became a crown colony administered by the Colonial Office.

The port lost some of its trade in the 1840's and 1850's when the British developed Hong Kong. The completion and opening of the Suez Canal in 1869, however, brought new importance to the area. As sailing vessels were replaced by steamships, Singapore served increasingly as a bunkering station. A period of sustained growth commenced in the 1870's. Harbor facilities were expanded, and after World War I a large naval base was constructed.

At the beginning of World War II the Japanese 25th Army under Lt. General Tomoyuki Yamashita landed on the beaches of Kota Bahru, Kelantan, in Malaysia, and by January 1942 had reached Johore Bahru on the mainland opposite Singapore. The British had provided for defense from a seaborne attacking force. Fortifications and artillery faced the sea. It was not considered likely that a hostile force would come down through the jungles of Malaya. But this is precisely what the Japanese did. In February, following British naval reverses with the loss of the *Prince of Wales* and the *Repulse*, they crossed to the island and the British capitulated. The Japanese occupation — a bloody period during which thousands of persons, mainly Chinese, were brutally murdered by the invaders — continued until the end of the war.

The civil administration was re-established in Singapore on April 1, 1946, and on that date Singapore became a separate crown colony with its own governor. The complexities of the political scene in the years immediately following World War II need not be traced here. At the beginning of the "Emergency" in Malaya in 1948 the authorities in Singapore acted promptly enough and with sufficient vigor to preserve a reasonable, if uneasy, calm.

In 1954 the People's Action Party (PAP) was founded. The party leader was Lee Kuan Yew. The Labour Front party emerged as victor in the elections of the following year and formed the government, the first under a new constitution. In the next few years Singapore moved closer to self-government — the British agreed that membership in the legislative assembly should be fully elective and elected ministers were given full responsibility in most areas. A joint Internal Security Council was established with equal representation of the British and Singapore governments and an additional single member designated by the Malaya government.

The Labour Front had no very strong program of action, excepting its highly vocal opposition to British colonial rule, and as its influence declined the PAP grew stronger. The party represented the left wing, and the Communists made an effort to gain control. Such success as they had was forfeited when Lim Yew Hock's Labour Front government arrested all but one of the pro-communist members of the PAP executive as subversives.

By 1955 the colony's elected ministers and legislature had largely assumed the responsibilities of government, excepting matters of defense and foreign affairs, and in 1959 Singapore became self-governing.

In the 1959 election the PAP gained an overwhelming majority of seats in the assembly and Lee Kuan Yew was made Prime Minister. The new government recognized the need for stability if foreign capital were to be attracted for increased industrialization, and larger markets for Singapore's industrial output created.

These and other factors pointed to the desirability of a merger with Malaya. As recounted elsewhere, the Malayans fretted over the left-leaning governments in Singapore and the Communist activity there. The possibility of an even more radical government assuming power occasioned an about-face in government policy in Kuala Lumpur in 1961. It now seemed safer to have Singapore inside the Federation, where it would be susceptible to some political control, than continuing as a threat outside it. After extended negotiations merger terms were arranged, and Singapore (as well as two Borneo territories) became part of the Federation of Malaysia when it was formed in 1963. The union was to exist for but two short years. After weathering the period of "confrontation" with Indonesia and internal political troubles, Singapore withdrew from the Federation in 1965 and became a sovereign, independent republic.

The reasons for withdrawal from the Federation were primarily racial in origin. The political leadership in Singapore was largely Chinese and felt that the federal government was too much dominated by the Malays. While mainland Malaysia possessed a Malay majority and a 40 per cent Chinese minority, in Singapore it was the other way around with 75 per cent of the populace Chinese and the remainder Malays and others.

Under the Singapore constitution every citizen, 21 or over, has one vote. Voting is compulsory. The Parliament is elected by secret ballot and has 58 members. The President of the Republic is elected by Parliament for a 4-year term, and he appoints the Prime Minister from among the members of Parliament. The President, on the advice of the Prime Minister, also appoints the Cabinet Ministers.

From 1965 onwards, Singapore has gone its own way as an independent republic, ever mindful of the need for cooperation with its two larger neighbors, Malaysia and Indonesia. The degree of stability and moderation in government which has been attained augurs well for the future. The island republic, with its great port, is realizing its aim of commercial leadership in Southeast Asia.

A Tour Around the Town

Singapore! What visions of the mysterious East are conjured up by the very word! The water front, old sailing ships, the smell of tar and the fresh salt breeze, Chinatown, Malay pirates, cargoes of pepper and spice, the China trade . . .

Today one will still find the waterfront, breathe the fresh sea air and visit tiny Chinese shops, but the old sailing vessels and pirates are decidedly in short supply. The rich heritage of the past is much in evidence in Singapore and while the newcomer to this bustling port city will find much of interest out of this past, he is likely to be equally impressed with the challenge of the future. Singapore is a forward-looking place.

The city is situated on the south side of the island. Half the population of the country live here, and it is the capital of the republic. It commands the Strait of Malacca, which connects the Indian Ocean with the South China Sea. The island of Sumatra and the Indonesian Archipelago lie across the Strait to the south.

How to describe the city itself? Architecturally one finds century-old shop-houses and some examples of the old colonial bungalows in the older sections juxtaposed with modernistic office buildings and modern apartments built by the Housing and Development Board for the half-million people who now live in them. There are Malay houses built on stilts, rambling tropical homes and Chinese bungalows. The overall impression is that of a "modern" metropolis. True, there are hundreds of little Chinese shops and there are older sections where urban renewal hasn't yet arrived. But the scores of modern office buildings, luxury hotels and impressive government buildings dominate the visitor's first impression.

The Singapore River cuts through the city. On the one side are the business district shops and the Chinese community. On the other,

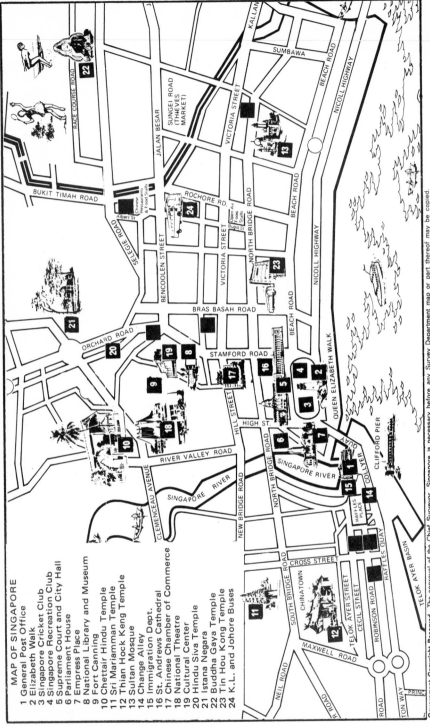

MAP OF SINGAPORE

1 General Post Office
2 Elizabeth Walk
3 Singapore Cricket Club
4 Singapore Recreation Club
5 Supreme Court and City Hall
6 Parliament House
7 Empress Place
8 National Library and Museum
9 Fort Canning
10 Chettair Hindu Temple
11 Sri Mariamman Temple
12 Thian Hock Keng Temple
13 Sultan Mosque
14 Change Alley
15 Immigration Dept.
16 St. Andrews Cathedral
17 Chinese Chamber of Commerce
18 National Theatre
19 Cultural Center
20 Hindu Siva Temple
21 Istana Negara
22 Buddha Gaya Temple
23 Tin Hou Kong Temple
24 K.L. and Johore Buses

Government Copyright Reserved. The approval of the Chief Surveyor, Singapore is necessary before any Survey Department map or part thereof may be copied.

Thai-American Publishers, 103 Park Avenue, New York

Singapore Skyline

Queen Elizabeth Walk

Singapore City Hall

Supreme Court

National Parliament

Victoria Memorial Hall

Raffles Landing Site

Singapore River

Raffles Statue at Empress Place

Raffles Place

Siang Lim Siang Si (Buddhist) Temple

Sri Mariamman Temple

Lion Dance Festival

Author at the Landing Site

government buildings, the esplanade by the sea, hotels and more shops. The residential areas are further out and are especially nice around the University of Singapore and the Botanical Gardens.

Long under British rule, almost everyone in the city speaks or understands some English. While in some of the more "native" sections the shop fronts may display only Chinese signs, elsewhere the English language is much in evidence.

Whether the visitor who is in a hurry takes a quick guided tour, or, with more leisure, strikes out for himself to see the sights, there are certain to be a number of places which he cannot afford to miss.

The General Post Office, which is at the mouth of the Singapore River, provides an excellent reference point. Only a few steps away, on a promontory projecting into the river estuary, is Merlion Park. At its extreme end, overlooking the water, is the 26-foot high Merlion — head and upper body of a lion joined to the body and tail of a fish. Water spouts from the mouth of this curious denizen and at night it is brightly illuminated as a colorful attraction for the casual stroller along Elizabeth Walk.

This lovely esplanade stretches along the waterfront from the river bridge in front of the G.P.O. to the Cenotaph by Stamford Road. Singaporeans are most partial to this beautiful promenade and will be seen here at all hours of the day and well into the evening. The walk is almost a mile long and was constructed on reclaimed land. There are benches along the quay for those who prefer to sit rather than stroll, perhaps to enjoy a tropical sunset across the water. Well-kept flowering shrubs, bougainvilleas, venerable old rain-trees and other tropical greenery provide a veritable oasis from the noise and hurry of nearby city streets. Connaught Drive runs along the Walk, and crossing it one stands at the edge of a vast green field with the Singapore Cricket Club at one end and the Singapore Recreation Club at the other.

The Supreme Court and City Hall buildings lie directly across the field. The former is a large domed structure with Corinthian columns. City Hall contains the offices of the Prime Minister and is the seat of government. Of particular interest inside the building is the surrender chamber wherein, on September 12, 1945, General Susheiro Itagaki, on behalf of the Supreme Japanese Commander in the area, surrendered all Japanese armed forces in Southeast Asia (excepting the Philippines) to Lord Louis Mountbatten, Supreme Allied Commander for Southeast Asia. Outside the chamber there are contemporary newspaper accounts, maps and pictures of the war on display. Inside, in the darkened chamber, one views a short motion picture film of the surrender with a sound track of the actual proceedings. Then the lights are turned up to reveal lifelike wax figures of Mountbatten, Itagaki and the other high-ranking military officials seated around the surrender tables — an impressive and moving tableau recreating the actual scene of the surrender.

A few steps along St. Andrews Road and across High Street one comes to Parliament House and other government buildings including those housing the Department of Immigration and the Board of Commissioners of Currency.

Nearby, on the east bank of the river, is the historic landing site of Sir Stamford Raffles who stepped ashore here in January 1819. The spot is marked by a gleaming white statue of Raffles, which looks out upon a city that since his day has developed "from an obscure fishing village to a great seaport and modern metropolis" as is inscribed in four languages on a plaque at the base of the monument. The river here is lined with river boats. They are so numerous and so tightly packed that one wonders how there is room to navigate at all.

A few hundred yards from the landing site are the great clock tower and Victoria Theatre and Hall which dominate Empress Place. Numerous exhibitions, celebrations, concerts and other entertainments and meetings are from time to time held here.

Moving now out a bit from the city center toward Orchard Road, a busy thoroughfare along which there are some of the newest of the luxury hotels, the visitor may well be inclined to spend some time at the National Library and Museum. The beginnings of the Museum collections go back to 1832, almost to the beginning of the city. They present the natural history and ethnology of Southeast Asia. The various exhibits of animals, weapons, boats, homecrafts, paintings and archaeological findings are as informative as they are interesting.

Fort Canning Hill, with its first Government House (now headquarters of the Singapore Garrison), and King George V Park are in this same area. The National Theatre and Van Kleef Aquarium are on the Park grounds, and there are numerous paths through the gardens and tropical trees for a pleasant walk.

Back on Orchard Road there is an interesting Hindu temple only a short distance from Fort Canning. Still another, no more than a mile away, is the Chettair Hindu Temple built more than a century ago. It houses a Hindu goddess, and at certain holy times of year processions come from all over the island to take part in religious rites here. If the Chettair Temple is the richest in Singapore, Sri Mariamman Temple (across the city on South Bridge Road) is the oldest. It was built in 1827 and extensively reconstructed in 1850. It is unusual because of its tower (*gopuram*) which is elaborately decorated with miniature replicas of Hindu deities.

A Chinese temple, Thian Hock Keng, is only a few streets away from Sri Mariamman and is the most important and oldest Hokkien temple in Singapore. Its origins date from 1821, and its chief deity image — the Queen of Heaven — was transported here from China in 1840.

For Muslim faithful there are a number of mosques, the most noteworthy architecturally being the Sultan Mosque on North Bridge Road near Arab Street. A number of small shops close by offer Indian and Batik fabrics and embroideries.

Mount Faber is less than six kilometers from the G.P.O. and well worth a visit. From its beautiful grounds there are magnificent views of the city and harbor. The tropical island resort of Sentosa seems very near, and in the distance the eye can scan the Rhio Archipelago of Indonesia. It is possible to see three countries from the Mount — Singapore, Malaysia and Indonesia.

But a scant few of the places even the casual visitor will probably see in Singapore have been noted. Scarcely any mention has been made of this great port city's harbor. The harbor, with its busy wharves and cavernous *godowns* (warehouses), is crowded with vessels of every description. There are ocean liners, cruise and cargo ships, naval vessels, spice boats, Chinese junks and sampans.

Mere listing of some other interesting places in and around the city is suggestive of what awaits the traveler who has the time and inclination to visit them: Botanic Gardens, Changi Beach, House of Jade, Soochow Garden and the Siong Lim Buddhist Temple, the crocodile farms, Jurong Bird Park, Thieves' Market along Rochore Canal, Tiger Balm Gardens, Change Alley and Raffles Place.

A drive northwest out of the city along Bukit Timah Road and then along Woodlands Road to the causeway takes one across the entire island. Stops can be made at the forest reserve and at the Mandai Orchid Gardens on Mandai Road.

Well to the north there is a small rubber plantation along the roadway, and it is easy to observe here how the trees are cut and the latex collected. Perchance, if it is midday, the shade of the rubber trees will provide a cool haven from the hot sun. It is quite possible that this plantation will in the not distant future give way to some commercial or industrial use of the land. That is the trend on the island today.

The Kranji War Memorial stands on a quiet hillside overlooking the Straits of Johore. Here the names of 24,000 men and women who fought and died during World War II are commemorated, and in the surrounding cemetery another 4,000 rest under individual head-stones.

APPENDIX

Rulers of the Chakri Dynasty

King Yodfah Chulaloke	Rama I	1782-1809
King Lert-Lah	Rama II	1809-1824
King Nang Klao	Rama III	1824-1851
King Mongkut	Rama IV	1851-1868
King Chulalongkorn	Rama V	1868-1910
King Vajiravudh	Rama VI	1910-1925
King Prajadhiphok	Rama VII	1925-1934
King Ananda Mahidol	Rama VIII	1934-1946
King Bhumibol Adulyadej	Rama IX	1946-

Periods in Thai History

Dvaravati	5th-7th century
Srivijaya	7th-11th century
Lopburi	10th-13th century
Chiangsaen	11th-13th century
Sukhothai	13th-14th century
Ayutthaya	14th-18th century
Ratanakosin	18th-20th century